CAUGHT IN THE ACT

MODERN DRAMA
AS PRELUDE TO THE GOSPEL

CAUGHT IN THE ACT

MODERN DRAMA
AS PRELUDE TO THE GOSPEL

by John Van Zanten

THE WESTMINSTER PRESS
Philadelphia

ISBN 0-664-24925-6   Nov 30 71

LIBRARY OF CONGRESS CATALOG CARD No. 72-158573

BOOK DESIGN BY
DOROTHY ALDEN SMITH

Published by The Westminster Press ®
Philadelphia, Pennsylvania

PRINTED IN THE UNITED STATES OF AMERICA

CONTENTS

PREFACE

IN THE FIRST PART OF CHAPTER 1, JOHN VAN ZANTEN describes our cultural inheritance. We are the heirs of centuries of what he has called "scientific materialism." We are also heirs, he says, of an intense spiritual anguish, created by a preoccupation with the material and a corresponding neglect of the spiritual.

He cites examples of dramatists who reflect that spiritual anguish. Central to their plays is the theme that, in a mechanistic universe, man must live by illusions or be destroyed.

But in the second part of the chapter, the author describes a new development in our culture. The discoveries and insights of modern physicists have shattered the world view of classical physics. Men no longer regard the universe as a vast machine, clanking along according to fixed and discernible laws. There is room, there is necessity, for faith and mystery—and hence new breathing room for the human spirit.

Contemporary dramatists, says Van Zanten, are reflecting this cultural change. Although they remain heirs of the age of scientific materialism and determinism, they are also heralds of the new age of indeterminism and mystery. They have begun to explore areas that once were closed to them. They are raising questions about sin and death, freedom and grace, time and eternity.

But because these writers are not only heralds of a new age but also heirs of the old, we cannot expect them to sound a clear note. We must expect to find them still speaking of illusions, of despair, and of absurdity—as well as of sin and of grace.

O'LINN McGUIRE, JR.

FOREWORD

THE SERIES OF ESSAYS THAT FOLLOW ARE AN ATTEMPT TO present the insights and findings of modern dramatists about the era in which we live. It is becoming more and more clear to us that we exist today in a time between cultures, between ages. The old values and institutions have broken down and the new have not yet appeared. It is a time of bewilderment and confusion. Life seems to be without direction or purpose. The absurd is king.

The playwrights, being sensitive emotionally and intellectually to what is happening, help us in their plays to understand what it means to be alive today . . . to face the problems of freedom and responsibility, guilt and forgiveness, death and disillusion, time and eternity, violence and rebellion, the abstract and the concrete, body and spirit, faith and grace. The writers do not have "messages" for us; they concentrate on the situation, on the human questions which are current and yet constant in human history. We do not find the Christian gospel in their plays, but we do find a *prelude* to the gospel. If the Christian faith is to speak to our condition, it must understand that condition. In these plays the modern "condition" is defined.

These essays came into being originally as presentations for discussion in the Seminars for Young Pastors and the Seminars for Experienced Pastors organized and administered by the Division of Continuing Education of the Board of Christian Education of The United Presbyterian Church U.S.A. I am most grateful to the pastors across the nation who have entered into these discussions over the past ten years and have enlarged many of the insights found in these pages. It is impossible for me to distinguish between my original ideas and the important additions that have been given to me by my colleagues.

It is my hope that these essays will persuade the reader to read modern dramas and to attend the theater in order to be enriched by the genius of the playwrights.

I would like to express my gratitude, also, to Dennis E. Shoemaker and John C. Purdy for suggesting that I put these presentations into essay form and for publishing many of them in the magazines *Crossroads* and *Trends*.

JOHN VAN ZANTEN

1
A NEW AGE
OF THE SPIRIT

FOR THREE HUNDRED AND FIFTY YEARS THE THINKING OF Western man has been dominated by scientific materialism. What is "material" has been carefully separated from what is "spiritual," and man has concerned himself primarily with the material. Only matter—that which can be observed, tested, analyzed, taken apart and put together again—has been recognized as real. The universe has been viewed as a machine governed by unchangeable scientific laws. Classical physics from Isaac Newton to the twentieth century has proclaimed the unity and predictability of nature.

Man, made bold and confident by these scientific assumptions, has used his understanding of physical laws to develop an industrial-technological culture. The latest advances in automation and cybernetics are directly related to the original discoveries and assertions of Newton and others. The preoccupation of Western man has been to find the cause, determine the development, and control the result.

As a consequence of this mechanistic view, we live today in a world groping for direction and meaning. We know the mechanics; we do not know the goal. The radical theologians express our bewilderment by announcing that "God is dead." Scientific materialism has no place for deity, no awareness of the spirit. There are no absolute truths, no ultimate values. All is flux. Men have sought the causes of everything and have turned away from any idea of purpose in the universe. A world view has arisen which holds that the universe is neutral to human values. The Princeton philosopher W. T. Stace has said: "The world which surrounds us is nothing but an immense spiritual emptiness. It is a dead universe. We do not live in a universe which is on the side of our values. It is completely indifferent to them." [1]

In the twentieth century, the enthusiasm for scientific discovery and technological advance has become tempered with anxiety and dread as the meaninglessness and spiritual emptiness of life in a morally neutral universe become increasingly clear to us. We have become "the hollow men." For modern man, who lives in the realm of causality, life has no meaning. An essayist in a recent issue of *Time* notes, "Man . . . is a creature trapped between two voids, prenatal and posthumous, on a shrinking spit of sand he calls time." [2] This modern man knows what it is to be estranged from his fellows, to be alone in the midst of his family, to be unable to communicate his

[1] From "Men Against Darkness," in *Atlantic*, September, 1948 Copyright 1948 by The Atlantic Monthly Company.
[2] From an essay in *Time*, July 8, 1966, "The Modern Theater or the World as a Metaphor of Dread." © 1966 Time, Inc.

ideas and feelings to others, to bear the heavy weight of physical objects. Man lives in a spiritual isolation, facing death, the final absurdity.

The artists and writers of any culture are the ones who first pick up signs of spiritual anguish. They are more sensitive than the rest of humanity to the world about us. These men suffer and express our common pain. They hold the mirror up to nature and to man. They do not give answers. We cannot look to them for a reinterpretation of the gospel of Christ in our age. But they do tell us what it is like to live in this scientific-technological age. Marshall McLuhan, former Director of the Center for Culture and Technology at the University of Toronto, states: "I think of art, at its most significant, as a DEW line, a Distant Early Warning system that can always be relied on to tell the old culture what is beginning to happen to it." [3]

McLuhan points out that "painters and artists have been quite conscious of their jobs as teaching people how to perceive the world they live in . . . probing the environment." When we do not like what the artists and writers are telling us about ourselves, we insist that we cannot understand them and that their work is absurd and ridiculous. The hostility of men and women today toward modern art and literature may be what Oscar Wilde described as "the rage of Caliban at seeing his own face."

For the past seventy-five years the artist, as dramatist

[3] As quoted in "Is Technology Taking Over?" by Charles E. Silberman, in *Fortune,* February, 1966. © 1966 Time, Inc.

and novelist, has been telling us about our human condition. The burden of his message is that scientific-technological man has inherited a world view that he cannot morally or spiritually endure. The artist portrays man as a being who creates and clings to illusions in order to avoid facing the absurdity of reality. The dramatists, from Henrik Ibsen to Edward Albee, have written of the need for illusions and the tragedy when the illusions collapse, as they must, under the pressure of reality. Modern tragedy is not heroic, it is pathetic. Its central character is not a hero, but a victim.

HENRIK IBSEN/*The Wild Duck*

Ibsen was the first of the major modern playwrights to sense and portray the effect of scientific technology on the human spirit. *The Wild Duck* is often considered his *Hamlet*. The symbolism of the wild duck is psychologically fascinating. In the play, an old hunter says that when a wild duck is shot and wounded, it dives to the bottom of the lake. "They shoot to the bottom as deep as they can get . . . and bite themselves fast in the tangle and seaweed—and all the devil's own mess that grows down there. And they never come up again." This is an excellent description of a neurotic, or even psychotic, personality. Such a person dives to the bottom of his unconscious, as deep as he can get, and there he bites himself fast in all the illusions, obsessions, and fantasies that are there. It is a labor of Hercules to persuade him to let loose his grip and to surface once more in the realm of conscious rationality. There are many who never come up again.

In Ibsen's play, Hialmar Ekdal is a man who lives by illusions. His life would be too painful for him if he were forced to face reality. He has hopes of success; but the truth is that he possesses no talent of any sort. He is married and has a daughter whom he loves above all; but the truth is that the child is the product of a union between his wife and another man. A knowing physician —and good friend—keeps him going by encouraging the illusion that he is an inventor and will someday astound the world with his genius. The doctor also assures him the little girl is a perfect daughter.

But into the scene comes a man who insists that reality must be faced. Truth must be told. He explains to the doctor that the would-be inventor cannot begin to live his real life until he faces the truth about himself and the facts about his daughter. The physician replies sharply, "Rob the average man of his life-illusion, and you rob him of his happiness at the same stroke."

The "reality seeker" has his way, however, and the dreaming inventor is forced to face the facts about himself and the child. The result is that the girl kills herself in despair, and the man is left without hope and in agony of spirit. Ibsen seems to be saying that illusion is necessary if life is to continue with any vitality.

EUGENE O'NEILL/*The Iceman Cometh*

This same realization is found in all the plays of America's foremost dramatist, Eugene O'Neill. He once remarked to a friend that the quality of a man's life depends upon the quality of his illusions. In his famous analysis of illusion and reality, *The Iceman Cometh*, O'Neill shows us a group of "lost" individuals who spend their days in the back room of a waterfront bar. Between drinks of cheap liquor, they describe to one another their pipe dreams. Each has the illusion that he will one day sober up, clean up, put on his good suit, and return to an active, successful life. They swap lies and carefully avoid facing the truth about themselves.

One day, into the back room comes Teddy Hickey, a salesman who joins them once a year to get drunk. They have been looking for him with high anticipation because he buys good whiskey for everyone and tells them the latest jokes from the smoking cars across the country. But when Hickey arrives, he is cold sober and, like an evangelist, preaches to them that they must stop living with lies, with pipe dreams, and face reality. He is able to persuade them to clean up and go out into the world again to recapture their former supposedly successful careers. The men try. But at the end of one day they are all back in the bar and in despair. Not one of them has been able to make any headway in the real world. Their hopelessness is now complete. They complain that even the liquor doesn't make them drunk any more. They accuse Hickey of destroying them. Only their pipe dreams and the false courage of drink have made it possible for them to face their inner emptiness.

Two policemen appear and arrest Hickey for the murder of his wife. He asks for time to explain to his "friends" how this happened. In a twenty-minute soliloquy, he tells the story of his life with Evelyn, his wife. They loved each other dearly. He was unfaithful to her time and again, but she always forgave him. His drinking made her miserable, but she refused to turn against him and always bravely told him that she knew he would conquer his temptations and that they would be happy together. Finally, when he could endure her forgiveness and faithfulness no longer, he killed her—so that she would not have to suffer any longer for his sins. He tells the men that he killed her because he "loved" her so much. But he surprised himself by shouting obscenities at her after the shot was fired. As Hickey is taken away by the police, he calls to his drinking companions, "No, I never . . . I loved Evelyn."

The men realize that Hickey has been living by his own pipe dream. They return to their drinking and find that liquor again takes its desired effect. The play closes with the men repeating their lies to one another, once more safe in the realm of their illusions.

The dramatist is telling us that tragedy comes for man when his "life illusions" are broken and he is forced to face a reality that is absurd. The human spirit cannot abide a universe that is indifferent. Escape from this indifference is sought in alcoholism, drug addiction, sexual promiscuity, obsessive work patterns, and firmly held illusions.

ARTHUR MILLER/*Death of a Salesman*

Arthur Miller's *Death of a Salesman* is a dramatic master-piece that unfolds for us the tragedy of what happens to a man when his basic illusion fails him. Willy Loman, a salesman like Teddy Hickey, has built his life on this pipe dream: "The man who makes an appearance in the business world, the man who creates personal interest, is the man who gets ahead. Be liked and you will never want." [4]

For many years his illusion has worked. He has been liked; he has traveled from city to city on a smile and a shoeshine; he has made sales. And he has brought up his two sons with the same illusion. For a time they believe him and are proud of him and think he will solve all problems for them in school and in life.

But then comes the day when the illusion fails. Willy is still "very well liked in Hartford," but he can't sell anything. He fights to keep his illusion alive in the face of harsh reality. His son, Biff, now a grown man who has failed at every undertaking despite his father's glowing descriptions of his future, comes home and holds up the truth before his father:

> The man don't know who we are! The man is gonna know! We never told the truth for ten minutes in this house! . . . I stole myself out of every good

[4] From *Death of a Saleman*, by Arthur Miller. Copyright 1949 by Arthur Miller. Reprinted by permission of The Viking Press, Inc.

job since high school! . . . And I never got any-
where because you blew me so full of hot air I could
never stand taking orders from anybody! . . . Pop!
I'm a dime a dozen, and so are you! . . . I am not
a leader of men, Willy, and neither are you. You
were never anything but a hard-working drummer
who landed in the ash can like all the rest of them!
I'm one dollar an hour, Willy! I tried seven states and
couldn't raise it. . . . I'm just what I am, that's all.[5]

As we hear Biff speak, we have the feeling that he may
be able to face his reality and endure life, but Willy cannot. When his illusion is broken, he kills himself, with a
further fond dream that his insurance money will give
his sons the backing they need for real success. The
playwright is saying to us that the truth makes men mad,
not free.

TENNESSEE WILLIAMS/*Cat on a Hot Tin Roof*

This same insight is found in the plays of Tennessee
Williams. His characters fall into death or madness when
their illusions are smashed. A clear portrayal of this idea
is found in Williams' *Cat on a Hot Tin Roof*. Maggie, the
"cat," is a woman who became suspicious of the relationship between her professional football player husband
and his best friend on the team. She decided to put the
friend to a test by attempting to seduce him. He failed
to respond to her, and she made it clear to him that he
was not a full man. By her action she forced him to face
the reality of his latent homosexuality. Unable to accept
this truth, he threw himself out of his hotel window to

[5] *Ibid.*

his death. Maggie, in trying to explain what happened, says to her angry husband, "I destroyed him, by telling him [the] truth."

EDWARD ALBEE/*Who's Afraid of Virginia Woolf?*

Edward Albee shows us the same relationship between illusion and reality in his famous *Who's Afraid of Virginia Woolf?* In the play we find a middle-aged couple, George and Martha, using every possible screen to hide from themselves the terror of life without meaning. The symbol of death, absurdity, purposelessness, is found in the name "Virginia Woolf." The real Mrs. Woolf was a noted British novelist of great sensibility whose life was haunted by madness and was ended by suicide. Her name is thus a murky sign for emptiness and the mystery of death. "Virginia Woolf" stands for the stark reality behind all frantic attempts to escape into illusion. Therefore, Albee closes his drama with a quiet scene between the once furiously battling couple:

GEORGE: Are you all right?
MARTHA: Yes. No.
GEORGE: (*Puts his hand gently on her shoulder; she puts her head back and he sings to her, very softly*)
                    Who's afraid of Virginia Woolf
                                    Virginia Woolf
                                    Virginia Woolf,
MARTHA: I . . . am . . . George. . . .[6]

[6] From *Who's Afraid of Virginia Woolf?*, by Edward Albee (Atheneum Publishers). Copyright © 1962 by Edward Albee.

Underneath all her bravado, drinking, seducing, fighting, scheming, and dreaming of a son she never had, Martha is terrified by the emptiness and absurdity of life in a universe that is indifferent.

These playwrights are "probing the environment" of our era. If we are to understand the world in which we live, we must listen carefully to them—even when such listening is painful. Since these dramatists are the heirs of an era that has accepted matter as the final reality, we cannot expect them to talk to us of revelation, of the breaking into our closed world of the grace of God. They are not aware of God, only of an immense spiritual emptiness. Their work can be only a prelude to the gospel.

But it is not all that simple, for the last few decades have witnessed a new development in our culture. It has become generally recognized that the world view shaped by classical physics is no longer tenable. The so-called "universal laws" work well for large bodies, but have been found not to apply to the microcosmic world of the new atomic physics. Einstein discovered that energy, not matter, is the more basic reality. Max Planck, in his study of light, found that it moves not only in waves but also in random particles. There is no strict predictability in dealing with energy and random particles. The nuclear physicist, Niels Bohr, has pointed out that the scientist is not really a spectator but actually a participant in his experiments. He sees what he is prepared to see. The free atom has never been observed in its natural habitat; it is studied as it performs in the cyclotron, a man-made apparatus.

Charles H. Townes, a Nobel Prize-winning physicist at M.I.T., tells us that the modern scientist works with hypotheses, educated guesses, and hopes to be able to demonstrate in the laboratory that his guesses are correct. He lives by "faith" that his insights will prove true in fact. Townes insists, "Faith is necessary for the scientist." He feels that a new close relationship is produced between science and religion. Each can learn from the other. Both seek order and meaning in the universe and in human life.

As the deterministic and mechanistic view of the universe of classical physics fades with the rise of atomic physics, modern man begins to perceive life with awe and wonder. The scientist no longer expects to know all causes and to be able to predict all results. He speaks of an ultimate mystery that stretches out into infinity beyond him. He expects to continue to find pieces of truth about that universe, but never the complete truth. Mystery has been restored to the universe, which can no longer be regarded as a machine.

The industrial-technological system of our era will continue to function and to expand. For practical purposes, classical physics with its universal laws will suffice. But the sensitive, thinking man of our generation knows that he must again deal with mystery, grace, and faith when he strives to comprehend reality. The period when absurdity was seen as the final reality is over. A new age of openness and awareness of the spirit has arrived.

Dramatists and novelists are responding to this new development. They are beginning to attempt to deal with such questions as the meaning of eternity and grace, the paradox of human freedom and slavery, the very real problem of sin, the threat of death, the reality of God, and the struggle to become genuinely part of the human family. It is to these attempts that this essay is directed. We shall consider the work of Thornton Wilder and Samuel Beckett, Eugène Ionesco, Albert Camus and Arthur Miller, Tennessee Williams, Edward Albee, William Hanley and LeRoi Jones, Tom Stoppard, Robert Bolt and Dale Wasserman, as these men struggle with the major spiritual questions of an age that is struggling to break the bonds of determinism and absurdity and to enter the new era of mystery and grace. The answers they suggest are not final, nor are they particularly Christian. But we can join them in the search for new understanding. They are part of the spiritual reformation and renewal of the mid-twentieth century.

Thus we find two responses by the writers of our day to the experience of our culture. The deterministic and mechanistic world view shaped by classical physics produced the reaction of meaninglessness in the minds of men. Writers have expressed this spiritual emptiness in the Theater of the Absurd and in the novels of existential nihilism. On the other hand, the openness and awareness of mystery made possible by the new atomic physics has involved them in a new search for spiritual realities. We see emerging the theater of compassion and the post-existentialist probing for lost meaning.

Of course, the two responses become intermingled in the work of serious writers, and we find ourselves confused by trying to follow two paths, seemingly leading in opposite directions. If the novelists and dramatists whom we encounter in this study do not always give a clear and certain message, it is because they are, as we are, caught in the midst of great cultural change. If nothing else, we can learn from them what it means to live in a time when the old is passing away and the new has already come. But we must first *listen* to what they have to teach us.

2
TIME
AND ETERNITY

THORNTON WILDER, AN AMERICAN, AND SAMUEL BECKETT, an Irishman who lives in Paris, seem on the surface to be separated by different experiences in life as well as by an ocean. Yet these two writers are dealing with the same problems of time and eternity. Both men possess a strange detachment from the world of daily life that allows them to view mankind from the perspective of another planet. Both look at life through a cosmic telescope. They try to help us to see and to understand what we miss in life around us.

THORNTON WILDER/*Our Town*

Wilder appears to be a calm, unmoved New Englander. His work seems to reflect this impassive stance; but as Hermine I. Popper remarks: "It masks but it cannot obliterate the ferment, the wonder and terror of life underneath." [7] Wilder has the austere, moral attitude of

[7] From "The Universe of Thornton Wilder," *Harper's Magazine,* June, 1965. Copyright © 1965 by Harper's Magazine, Inc.

a stern Puritan, but with a twentieth-century understanding of the unconscious elements, the irrational
drives, in human personality.

Wilder is not a man of the "moment," but one with an
acute sense of history. He knows where we have been as
a race, and he senses the direction in which we are
moving. He is concerned with what is continually important in human experience. Rather than writing of the
exotic and radically different, he insists, "I am interested
in those things that repeat and repeat and repeat in the
lives of millions." [8] He writes of family doings, small-
town events, birth, work, marriage, death. His attitude
toward these events and the people involved in them is
moral. As he says, "An artist is one who knows how life
should be lived at its best and is always aware of how
badly he is doing it." [9]

This American novelist and dramatist does not, like
so many of his contemporaries, work from inside our
culture and from inside his own experience; he is able
to remain, at least partially, outside. He invites us to join
him and look at our adventures on earth from a platform
somewhat above where we usually stand. With his help
we are able to achieve some degree of objectivity about
our lives. This enables us to understand better who we
are and what we are doing and to plan for the future
with some degree of confidence.

In an age that often seems to be crushing individuals
and forcing them into molds of conformity, Wilder is

[8] *Ibid.*
[9] *Ibid.*

concerned with what is happening to the individual: "I see myself making an effort to find the dignity in the trivial of our daily life, against those preposterous stretches which seem to rob it of any such dignity." [10]

In his famous play *Our Town,* he carefully inspects the daily life of a small New Hampshire town. He tells us many facts about Grover's Corners and its inhabitants. We live through a day in the homes of several families. We watch the age-old rituals of love and marriage. The last act deals with death, with the passing of a young wife and mother. The Stage Manager explains to the audience that this was the way people lived in New England in the opening years of the twentieth century, the way they grew up, married, lived, and died.

The young wife, Emily Webb Gibbs, dies at the time of the birth of her second child. Wilder has her join the other dead in the town cemetery. They sit on wooden chairs lined up in rows on the stage. As they talk with one another, we feel their growing detachment from their life on earth. Emily talks to her mother-in-law, who sits next to her. They talk of the improvements made on the farm. Suddenly, Emily breaks in with her agonized realization that living people just don't understand. Mrs. Gibbs agrees that this is so. Emily considers further and remarks that living people are, in a way, shut up in little boxes. A vast universe is spread out before them, but they see only what is in their little boxes.

In this scene the author is dealing with the matter of awareness. He recognizes that most of us go through life

[10] *Ibid.*

without really being aware of what is taking place. Child-hood vanishes and we are adults before we know it. Youth passes into middle age, and into old age, while we struggle, unseeing, with our daily problems. We are so busy and in such a hurry that we actually miss life itself, and the individual people who share it with us.

Are we able to recognize what is happening to us *at this moment?* Or are we so intent upon what we are planning for tomorrow and tomorrow that the *now* is lost? It is a constant human temptation to live "for the time when"—when our ship comes in, when the children grow up, when the new job materializes, when we can retire and do what we want. But life exists only *now,* not then. Thornton Wilder tries to help us to face this truth by letting us watch Emily return to life for one day on earth.

When Emily makes the discovery that she can return to life and live her days over again, she decides to try one day, her twelfth birthday. The Stage Manager makes the arrangements. Emily returns to her home as a child of twelve and watches with wonder as the routine life of the town unfolds around her.

She enters the kitchen for breakfast. Her mother is busy at the stove and pays little attention to her daughter. In the midst of her cooking duties, Mrs. Webb wishes Emily a happy birthday and tells her that there are surprises waiting for her on the table.

Emily is shocked and deeply hurt at her mother's lack of warmth. In an automatic way, she tells her mother that the family should not have provided gifts, and then, in agony, she turns to the Stage Manager and whispers to him that she cannot continue the scene.

Her mother, from the stove, continues to chatter away to her, saying that she wants her to eat a good breakfast in order to grow up into a strong girl. Mrs. Webb tells her that there is a present from her aunt and a postcard album from George Gibbs, who must have brought it over very early because it was on the doorstep with the milk.

Emily is greatly moved as she picks up the album. Overcome by her emotions and unable to stand any longer her mother's aloofness, she drops the album on the table and pleads with her mother to look at her for one moment as though she really saw her. Because it is a dream sequence, Mrs. Webb cannot hear and continues to stir the oatmeal.

Emily cries out to her mother that fourteen years have passed, that she is not a twelve-year-old girl but a grown-up woman, and now dead, that her mother is a grand-mother. Emily desperately tries to make her mother listen to her. The family is all together for a moment. Why can't they be happy? Why can't they just *look at one another?*

The mother hears nothing. She continues to talk about the birthday presents and tells Emily that her father has a surprise for her. As her father comes into the kitchen looking for her, Emily can stand it no longer. She rushes over to the Stage Manager and pours out all her anguish. She tells him she cannot go on, that everything goes so fast. She is amazed and horrified that people in life do not take time to look at one another. So much is going on and they never notice it.

Emily asks to be taken back up the hill to her grave. She gives the world one last look and bids farewell to the common, and wonderful, things of daily life: ticking clocks, a butternut tree, sunflowers, food, coffee, new-ironed dresses, hot baths, sleeping and waking up. She is overcome as she realizes the true wonders in our common life. She ponders for a moment and asks the Stage Manager if people ever realize life while they live it minute by minute. The Stage Manager shakes his head and says that perhaps saints and poets do—to some extent. Emily tells him that she is ready to go back to her grave. The full impact of this scene is felt by Hermine Popper when she writes:

> It is the compassionate moment that lingers in the memory, and informs *Our Town* with immortal life.
> Emily has to die in order to come down ultimately on the side of life.

Wilder would teach us to become aware of the eternal moment and of one another in time. The question can be asked of each of us, "Do *you* realize life while you are living it?" The saints and poets do. Is there anything of the saint or the poet in us? As we listen to this scene, we recognize that it is our spiritual and moral responsibility to arrest our headlong dash through life and to become aware of the *now*. Even at its most dreadful, life is a wonder and a mystery. The quality of life is determined by the measure of awareness that one possesses.

In both the Old and the New Testament, we are told

to love our neighbor. This does not mean to have a warm, sentimental feeling about him, but to "see" him as an individual. Emily longed for her mother to look at her *as though she really saw her*. The girl wanted her mother to express her true affection for her. But the mother was busy cooking breakfast, making plans for the day, remembering all the things she wanted to tell her daughter. So Emily, on her revisit to her twelfth birthday, felt like an object. She could not stand it. The lack of awareness among people drove her back to her grave.

Our Town may help us to understand something of the Christian faith, which enables us to see one another as individuals so important in the eyes of God that he sent his only Son into the world to die for each one. It is the failure to be aware of the infinite moment and the living individual that produces inhumanity, domestic conflict, and even war in the world. Do we really *see* the poor man, the member of the minority group, the drug addict, the bewildered adolescent, the frightened bully? By failing to *see* him, we drive him to revolt and violence. Awareness, as Wilder defines it, is close to what Jesus called love. We might sum up the drama: "Take time to look at one another."

SAMUEL BECKETT/*Waiting for Godot*

At first glance, Samuel Beckett does not seem to be in the same thought world with Thornton Wilder. Beckett is an Irishman who has spent most of his life in Paris. He writes in French and is a European both culturally and psychologically. He went through the emotional and spiritual exhaustion of World War II. As a member of the Resistance movement, he risked his life in underground activities when the Nazis overran France. The war itself produced anxiety and exhilaration, but it was followed by desperate weariness. Thoughtful men wondered if the sacrifices had been worthwhile. The ruthless bloodletting across Europe produced a disgust with human cruelty. The hate-filled slaughter of Jews in Nazi Germany and the hunting down of Jews in the surrounding countries during the years of German victories filled civilized minds with a vivid awareness of the irrational hostility to be found in human nature. The suffering of innocent persons, especially children, brought sensitive individuals to the place where they questioned the possibility of a loving God. Some men of compassion became atheists because they were compassionate.

Samuel Beckett was deeply moved by the scenes he witnessed and the stories he heard. The times stirred a powerful, creative impulse within him, and for five years he poured out a series of important works.

Beckett's plays are usually considered prime examples of the Theater of the Absurd. But Beckett is definitely part of the new wave of compassion. He is aware of the meaninglessness of life, but he is also aware of the reality of "grace." He perceives life with awe and wonder even as he struggles with its seeming absurdity. He possesses the same sense of ultimate mystery found in the minds of modern scientists. Beckett recognizes that man does not have answers; he wonders if answers are to be given from "outside."

A personal encounter with absurdity has colored his thinking. One day, in Paris, an underworld character stopped him on the street and asked him for money. When Beckett could not give him any, the stranger suddenly stabbed him. He was taken to the hospital with a perforated lung. After some time, Beckett recovered his health. He visited the knife-wielder in prison and asked the man why he had so suddenly stabbed him. His assailant answered, "I do not know."

Prominent among Beckett's plays is *Waiting for Godot*. In this drama we find the same two concerns of Thornton Wilder: the importance of time and the difficulty of communication among humans. *Waiting for Godot* was first presented in Paris in 1953. It was an immediate and great success. Translated into more than twenty languages, it has since been performed all over the world. Obviously, it is saying something that men of all cultures recognize. The play is serious in intent and yet filled with a wild kind of humor that keeps the audience laughing at the vaudevillian antics on stage. In the New York production, the noted American comedian, Bert Lahr, played one of the leading parts.

The setting of the play is desolate and sparse—"A country road. A tree. Evening." The tree has upon it one or two withered leaves. Two disheveled tramps, Estragon and Vladimir, appear and talk about various subjects. Sometimes they seem to be talking to each other, at other times only to themselves. The heart of their discussion is about the expected arrival of one Godot. They have been told that he will come that day, and they are waiting for him. While they wait, another couple appears on stage: a master, Pozzo, and a slave, Lucky. After much discussion and a long, incoherent lecture by Lucky, the newcomers disappear, and the tramps are left to continue their wait for Godot. At the close of the first act, a boy enters and tells them that Godot cannot come that day, but that he will come tomorrow. The two men talk of moving on and waiting no longer, but they do not move.

The second act is a repetition of the first. The tramps talk constantly, engage in some hilarious horseplay with their shoes and hats, and are visited again by Pozzo and Lucky. This time Pozzo is blind and seems to be led by Lucky. As the play comes to an end, the boy appears once more with the message that Godot is unable to come that day but will arrive "tomorrow." Again the men decide to leave, but do not move.

Who is Godot? Each one has to decide for himself. Alan Schneider, the director of the first American production, wrote to Beckett and asked for clarification about the identity of this awaited one. Beckett replied, "If I knew, I would have said so in the play." [11] This may mean that man waits for what he does not know.

[11] As quoted in *The Theatre of the Absurd,* by Martin Esslin (Anchor Book, Doubleday & Company, Inc.). Copyright © 1961 by Martin Esslin.

Each of us can supply objects for which we wait: our ship to come in, the children to grow up, the business promotion to be granted, retirement and the chance to do what we want. But beneath such personalized objects lies an unknown goal.

This brings us to Beckett's concern for time. Human beings are acutely aware of the passage of time that is experienced as waiting. As in *Our Town,* individuals tend to miss the importance of the moment as they wait for something momentous to happen— for Godot to come. Beckett may be saying that life is fulfilled in the moment, the ultimate instant of the present, rather than in the future. The Kingdom of God may be among us, not at the close of history.

As we consider this drama, we realize that the subject is not Godot, whoever or whatever that may be, but that it is *waiting* itself. Beckett is interested in the common human awareness of the passing of time. Man hopes that some event in his life will have ultimate meaning, a meaning that will make sense of the rest of his life. The rejection of this hope is found in the opening dialogue between the tramps:

ESTRAGON: Nothing to be done.
VLADIMIR: I'm beginning to come round to that opinion. All my life I've tried to put it from me, saying, Vladimir, be reasonable, you haven't tried everything. And I resumed the struggle. So there you are again.[12]

[12] From *Waiting for Godot,* by Samuel Beckett, translated from the original French text by the author. Copyright © 1954 by Grove Press, Inc. Used by permission of the publisher.

Trying to be reasonable, they face the fact that life is not going to be clearly outlined for them. They discuss suicide as an end of frustrated waiting, but they have neither the implements nor the courage for it.

This leads them to a consideration of grace. In Beckett's thought, grace is a power with meaning that breaks in upon life from beyond. When asked about the meaning of this play, Beckett has answered: "There is a wonderful sentence in Augustine. . . . 'Do not despair: one of the thieves was saved. Do not presume: one of the thieves was damned.'" [13] (The two thieves are those crucified on either side of Jesus.) In the play, we hear the two tramps talking of this Biblical event:

> VLADIMIR: One of the thieves was saved. It's a reasonable percentage. Gogo.
> ESTRAGON: What?
> VLADIMIR: Suppose we repented?
> ESTRAGON: Repented what?
> VLADIMIR: Oh. . . . We wouldn't have to go into the details.
> ESTRAGON: Our being born? [14]

Vladimir continues to show intense interest in the two thieves. For little reason, one was saved and one damned. At the moment of the crucifixion, one thief abused Jesus and the other rebuked his colleague. It might so easily have been the other way around. This event seems to mean to the two men that life is not redeemed by the reasonable, moral efforts of men, but through the strange workings of grace.

[13] As quoted in Esslin, *The Theatre of the Absurd.*
[14] Beckett, *Waiting for Godot.*

We might ask ourselves if we can take grace seriously until we have come to the place where we despair of human answers. As long as we think that somehow we can make sense out of our "waiting" on earth, we are walled off from the power of God seen as grace, faith, love, or participation in "the new being."

Pozzo and Lucky occupy and entertain the two tramps for a short time. Lucky performs a meaningless shuffle which is supposed to be a dance. He calls it "The Net." As Pozzo explains, "He thinks he is entangled in a net." [15] Another talent belonging to Lucky is the ability to "think." His "thinking" turns out to be a long harangue in a kind of learned gibberish. After the master and slave have left, the tramps engage in an exchange that gives us the mood of the drama:

> VLADIMIR: That passed the time.
> ESTRAGON: It would have passed in any case.
> VLADIMIR: Yes, but not so rapidly.
> *Pause.*
> ESTRAGON: What do we do now?
> VLADIMIR: I don't know.
> ESTRAGON: Let's go.
> VLADIMIR: We can't.
> ESTRAGON: Why not?
> VLADIMIR: We're waiting for Godot.
> ESTRAGON (*despairingly*): Ah! [16]

This repartee is obviously in the idiom of vaudeville patter. It makes no difference which one of the two speaks any of the lines; they are interchangeable. In

[15] *Ibid.*
[16] *Ibid.*

fact, in various parts of the drama, the same lines are reversed. Beckett is not seeking individuality or distinct characterization. Man, any man, can be distracted from his waiting by sideshows; but he is soon recalled by his associates to his central occupation.

Man's absorption with time and with future goals prevents him from living in spontaneity and fullness. When Pozzo appears for a second time, blind, he cries out:

> Have you not done tormenting me with your ac-
> cursed time! It's abominable! When! When! One
> day, is that not enough for you, one day he [Lucky]
> went dumb, one day I went blind, one day we'll
> go deaf, one day we were born, one day we shall
> die, the same day, the same second, is that not
> enough for you? . . . They give birth astride of a
> grave, the light gleams an instant, then it's night
> once more.[17]

Life is not meaningful in terms of duration. Before eternity, life is but an instant. Meaning is beyond time. In Christian faith, the resurrection—an event of eternal significance—appears from beyond the cruci-fixion. Those who waited for an earthly kingdom with Jesus as ruler, with places for his favorites on his right and left, were disappointed. There are those who occupy themselves with waiting for the end of the world, the judgment of God, and the salvation of the righteous few; they, too, are doomed to disappointment. The ways of God are not the ways of men. The meaning of life is

17 *Ibid.*

not disclosed by the thinking of men or by their waiting for a new kind of knowledge. Meaning is revealed in a *moment* of existence. Men live by grace; they are grasped by faith; they are *surprised* by meaning.

In *Our Town,* Emily had been so intent upon waiting for marriage, her own home, children, her future, that she had not been aware of what was happening each moment. After her few minutes of complete awareness, she faced the fact that she, like all of us, had lived without realizing what was going on. She had been blind and deaf to most of what was happening around her.

In *Waiting for Godot,* the two tramps are so intent upon waiting that they are not aware of life, of one another, or of the gifts of grace. Always waiting, one says: "Tonight perhaps we shall sleep in his place, in the warmth, dry, our bellies full, on the straw. It is worth waiting for that, is it not?" [18]

Both Thornton Wilder and Samuel Beckett plead with us to realize life while we live it.

[18] As quoted in Esslin, *The Theatre of the Absurd.*

3
FREEDOM
AND SECURITY

ANOTHER EXPATRIATE LIVING IN PARIS IS EUGÈNE IONESCO. Like Samuel Beckett, he finds the French city and language congenial to his personality and work. Also like Beckett, Ionesco is usually considered a member of the Theater of the Absurd. He thinks of himself as an existentialist, one who examines life as he finds it in his own experience and who has made a commitment to a particular way of life. Ionesco has committed himself to the humanizing of modern existence.

Ionesco believes that the industrial-technological age with its center in the jungle-city is dehumanizing man. Brainwashing takes place in the educational system, the mass media, the home, and the marketplace. People are taught to adjust, not to think. Brains and creativity are suspect. New ideas tend to be considered subversive. The "good" citizen is ordinary in every way. He may have a Walter Mitty fantasy life, but he carefully keeps his dreams to himself.

Man is also dehumanized by being cut off from his

self-transcendent qualities. He loses in himself the image of God and becomes a copy of intelligent nature. This dehumanization makes life absurd. Ionesco says:

> Absurd is that which is devoid of purpose. . . . Cut off from his religious, metaphysical, and transcendental roots, man is lost; all his actions become senseless, absurd, useless.[19]

Ionesco struggles against the absurd in life. He believes that life ought to have transcendent meaning and that man ought to have humanity; he ought to *be* man and not a distortion of mankind, neither a manikin nor a monster.

Because we live in a period between ages, because the period of the steam engine is over and the thermonuclear era is beginning, the social structures and political systems familiar to us have collapsed. Threatened by anarchy, we are tempted to pretend that the old structures are still viable. An open, revolutionary period in history drives many to live in illusions of past security. Ionesco asks us if we are able to face the collapse of old structures and to move into an unknown future with courage and some measure of confidence.

The "death of God" movement is a way of stating this situation theologically. The religious structures that men erected to give order to life have collapsed. The "god" worshiped as a part of the old structure is, indeed, dead. He never did exist, but we are just finding that out. We can refuse to face this discovery and continue to worship the illusion, the "idol"; or we can enter

[19] *Ibid.*

the new period of wrestling with mystery and the unknown.

In this connection it must be remembered that the heart of the Biblical message is that God reveals himself to us; we do not discover him by our efforts and "prove" his existence. Just because we *need* God, we cannot fabricate him. And God does not reveal himself when we snap our fingers, or even when we cry out to him with broken hearts and agonized spirits. He reveals himself "in the fullness of time." This is not our time, but his.

At this time between ages, a debate is raging between the traditionalists and the existentialists. As the historian Marshall W. Fishwick puts it: "The former insist on keeping the inherited house tidy; the latter on discarding it and building anew. That we face unprecedented political and intellectual crises, no one denies. But what should our response and attitude be? Should we guard the fort or abandon it for the frontier?" [20]

Ionesco decided to abandon the fort for the frontier. To set out for the frontier is to seek authentic human existence. To be authentic as a human being, one must escape abstractions, circumlocutions, and pomposity. To be on the frontier means action and involvement.

[20] From "Diagnosing the American Dream," in *Saturday Review*, Dec. 21, 1963. © 1963 by Saturday Review Inc.

EUGÈNE IONESCO / *Rhinoceros*

In his play *Rhinoceros*, Eugène Ionesco is doing battle with inauthentic existence. He feels that mankind is in danger of being transformed into thick-skinned, insensitive, lumbering rhinos. But he does battle with a shout of laughter. As the American playwright William Saroyan points out, "Ionesco laughs steadily, and the ache of absurdity, failure, and despair is felt, if it is felt at all, in the midst of a kind of hyena laughter, a voiceless laughter, a laughter that is noisy only in the lungs and mouth of the astonished spirit." [21] This laughter should not lead us into thinking that Ionesco is a harmless comedian. For as Saroyan warns: "Watch out for those anarchists whose only bomb is the word. They are writing the writing on the wall. Listen carefully to everything they say. You can always read your paper, too." [22]

Rhinoceros comes out of Ionesco's experience with the fascist movements before and during the Second World War. He left his native Romania for Paris in 1938, when he noticed more and more of his acquaintances joining the Iron Guard, a fascist organization. In 1960, Ionesco said of his personal experience:

I remembered that in the course of my life I have been very much struck by what one might call the current of opinion, by its rapid evolution, its power of contagion, which is that of a real epidemic. Peo-

[21] From "Ionesco," by William Saroyan, in *Theatre Arts*, July, 1958. Copyright 1958 by Theatre Arts Council.
[22] *Ibid.*

ple allow themselves suddenly to be invaded by a
new religion, a doctrine, a fanaticism. . . . At such
moments we witness a veritable mental mutation. I
don't know if you have noticed it, but when people
no longer share your opinions, when you can no
longer make yourself understood by them, one has
the impression of being confronted with monsters
—rhinos, for example. They have that mixture of
candor and ferocity. They would kill you with the
best of consciences. And history has shown us during the last quarter of a century that people thus
transformed not only resemble rhinos, but really become rhinoceroses.[23]

The rhinoceros is for Ionesco a symbol of inauthentic human existence as well as for security-minded
traditionalism. He wrote *Rhinoceros* to show man caught
between his desire for freedom and his desire for security.

The central character in the play is Berenger. He is
described by Henry Hewes, the drama critic of the
Saturday Review, as "a timid soul naïve enough to
believe in morality, public responsibility, friendship, and
marriage, and Christian enough to give every other
human being the benefit of the doubt."

Berenger is an individualist by default. He would like
to be an adjusted, accepted member of society, but he
is somehow unable to make the grade. He is not well-
groomed enough to enter society, he is not efficient or
ambitious enough to succeed in business, he is not

[23] From an interview with Eugène Ionesco by Claude Sarraute
in *Le Monde,* Jan. 13, 1960, as quoted in Esslin, *The Theatre of
the Absurd.*

thoughtful or creative enough to be a respected eccentric. He tries halfheartedly to fit in with the customs and traditions of his community, but he fails.

The drama opens in the square of a small provincial town in France. It is a Sunday morning, and we find Berenger meeting his well-dressed and groomed friend, Jean. A conservative gentleman of the old school, Jean is disgusted with Berenger's appearance. Berenger is unshaven, his shirt is soiled, he has lost his necktie, his shoes are unshined, his suit is wrinkled and has white dust on the shoulders. It is obvious that he has drunk too much the night before. Jean berates him for all his obvious shortcomings and peremptorily orders him to clean himself up and change his ways. Berenger accepts all the criticisms and promises to do better. He wants to win his friend's approval.

Jean, who seems to embody everything that Berenger lacks, suggests that his slovenly friend also try to improve his mind by attending lectures and visiting the museum. Berenger agrees to do it. Jean is sure of himself, self-righteous to the degree of pomposity, and arrogant. We feel that he is a thoroughgoing fraud, but the naïve Berenger is impressed by him. The scene is suddenly interrupted by a rhinoceros charging down the main street of the town directly past the café where the two men are sitting.

The townspeople rush out in agitation and surprise. Great excitement fills the square. A noisy discussion arises about how many horns the great beast had. An elderly logician patiently tries to reason out an answer to this dilemma. He engages in learned hairsplitting that is humorous and infuriating. The discussion ends with the logician stating that the important thing is to be able to ask the right question. A myriad of futile arguments on learned topics is ridiculed in this conversation. In the midst of the discussion, the rhino returns and thunders down the street in the opposite direction. The questions now become: Was it the same animal? Did it have one or two horns? Did the first beast have one horn and the second two? Is it a native of Africa or India?

During the second charge, the rhino tramples a pet cat to death. The reaction to this sad event is dramatic and overwhelming. The woman who owns the cat falls at once into profound, inconsolable grief. The townspeople join in the mourning. They loudly denounce the authorities who allow such tragedies to happen. A hastily assembled funeral procession, led by the local priest, moves mournfully toward the burial ground.

(This heightened reaction to the cat's death points to the false emotional values of a people who are unmoved by human tragedy. When we, in America, think of the money spent on luxuries for pet animals and the elaborate monuments raised in their memory in animal cemeteries, we can understand Ionesco's impatience and amusement at the furor over the cat's death.)

The event seems to act as a catharsis for all the pent-up emotions in the neighborhood. Berenger is the only one who seems unmoved by the accident. He is sorry for the woman who has lost her pet, and he is sorry the cat is killed, but he finds it simply impossible to become personally involved. This aloofness makes him suspect to the others in the town. Why can he not participate in their orgy of grief?

The scene changes to the business office where Berenger is employed as a clerk. He is the last one to reach his desk in the morning. There are others in the office who are on their way to larger responsibilities, but it is obvious that Berenger will be lucky to hold his present position. There is much talk about the sudden appearance of the rhinoceros in the town and the unfortunate demise of the cat.

While they are talking, a Mrs. Boeuf arrives and asks if her husband has been seen. He also is employed in this same office, but he has not appeared for work. She reports that she was followed to the office by a rhinoceros. She felt there was something familiar about him. It is discovered that he is in the lobby of the building. Mrs. Boeuf peers down the stairs at him and declares that it is her husband! She now recognizes him! The animal tries to come up the stairs, which break down under his weight. He trumpets and rushes off toward the open fields. Furthermore, it is discovered by a superficial count that thirty-two persons have become rhinoceroses!

(Ionesco witnessed this kind of transformation when Fascism was growing in Europe. Few were aware that it was taking place. The movement was subtle in the sense that individuals melted into a fascist group without seeming to change. One never knew whom to trust. Families were broken as the husband or wife accepted Fascism. When one understood what was taking place, it was as if certain individuals had joined a herd of animals, thick-skinned, greenish, boorish, rushing through town.)

Caught in their office without a stairway, the men call for the fire department and are rescued by ladders. Berenger, free for the day, goes to visit his friend, Jean, in the latter's rented room, a rather shabby dwelling for a man so natty in appearance. Jean is not feeling well. His skin itches, his forehead is lumpy, and he has a fever. He and Berenger argue about the number of horns on the rhinoceros' head. Berenger tries to appease his friend and to agree with him. But Jean will have none of it. He becomes angry and abuses Berenger. His personality begins to change; and before our eyes Jean becomes a snorting, stamping, trumpeting rhinoceros and rushes out of the room and the house to join the others. It is a shock to Berenger to watch Jean's transformation.

The final scene of the play takes place in Berenger's room, which is very much like Jean's. We find Berenger lying on his bed awakening from a nightmare in which he dreamed he had become a rhino. He sits up and gingerly feels his forehead for signs of a horn—or two horns. All seems well, and he is greatly relieved. He is visited by two people from his office—the pretty girl receptionist and an ambitious colleague. The other man soon leaves to join the rhinoceros herd. Berenger and Daisy are left alone as the last human beings who must face the new world and its lumbering inhabitants.

> BERENGER: Don't be frightened, my dear. We're to-
> gether—you're happy with me, aren't you? It's
> enough that I'm with you, isn't it? I'll chase all
> your fears away.

DAISY: Perhaps it's all our own fault.

BERENGER: Don't think about it any longer. We mustn't start feeling remorse. It's dangerous to start feeling guilty. We must just live our lives, and be happy. They're not spiteful, and we're not doing them any harm. They'll leave us in peace. You just keep calm and rest.[24]

(Ionesco is aware that opposition to Fascism did not arise immediately, because people felt that everything would work out all right. Just leave these troublesome individuals alone, and they will not trouble you, they thought. Every man has a "right" to be happy. It was too late when it was discovered that this "right" was not to be honored, and that the uniformed terrorists were going to break into the lives of everyone.)

The conversation continues:

DAISY: Let things just take their course. What can we do about it?

BERENGER: They've all gone mad. The world is sick. They're all sick.

DAISY: We shan't be the ones to cure them.

BERENGER: How can we live in the same house with them?

DAISY (*calming down*): We must be sensible. We must adapt ourselves and try and get on with them.

BERENGER: They can't understand us.

DAISY: They must. There's no other way.

BERENGER: Do you understand them?

---

[24] This quotation and those which follow from *Rhinoceros* are from *Rhinoceros and Other Plays*, by Eugène Ionesco, translated by Derek Prouse (Grove Press, Inc.). Copyright © 1960 by John Calder Publishers, Ltd. Used by permission of Grove Press, Inc.

DAISY: Not yet. But we must try to understand the
way their minds work, and learn their language.

(Again we find Ionesco echoing the sentiments he
heard expressed as the Fascists were coming to power
in Europe: "What can we do about it? . . . The world
is sick. . . . We must adapt ourselves. . . . We must
try to understand." It was this kind of talk that en-
couraged the totalitarians. They preached coexistence
until they were strong enough to devour their opponents.
Hitler talked "peace in our time" with the British Prime
Minister at Munich. The Allies tried to understand and
to work with the dictators until the panzer divisions
struck. The attempt to be "sensible" and to "adjust" was
prelude to defeat.)

As the scene continues, we hear Daisy changing her
sentiments and becoming appreciative of the virtues
of the rhinos. She suggests that perhaps Berenger and
she are the abnormal ones. She says: "Those are the
real people. They look happy. They're content to be
what they are. They don't look insane. They look very
natural. They were right to do what they did."

We can see that she is edging toward the realm of
the beasts. To Berenger, she insists, "It's the world that's
right—not you and me." Then she begins to see the
rhinos as beautiful, graceful creatures. She exclaims,
"They're like gods." It is not long before she slips away
from Berenger and joins the herd.

Berenger is now left alone. He is the only human
individual left in a world of rhinoceroses, who are
thundering and trumpeting about under his windows.
He speaks his thoughts:

Now I'm all on my own. (*He locks the door carefully, but angrily.*) But they won't get me. (*He carefully closes the window.*) You won't get me! (*He addresses all the rhinoceros heads.*) I'm not joining you; I don't understand you! I'm staying as I am. I'm a human being. A human being.

After these brave words, Berenger considers what he ought to do, and concludes that it is his responsibility to change these beasts back to human beings:

The only solution is to convince them—but convince them of what? Are the changes reversible, that's the point? Are they reversible? It would be a labour of Hercules, far beyond me. In any case, to convince them you'd have to talk to them. And to talk to them I'd have to learn their language. Or they'd have to learn mine. But what language do I speak? What is my language? Am I talking French? Yes, it must be French. . . . What am I saying? Do I understand what I'm saying? Do I?

Berenger quails before the thought of trying to reach the ferocious animals, learning their language, convincing them of their folly, to save the world from violence. The more he thinks of the difficulties involved, the more he begins to wonder if the beasts are not right after all. One answer is to join them. He looks into a mirror and speaks his vacillating mind:

I'm not good-looking. They're the good-looking ones. I was wrong! Oh, how I wish I was like them! I haven't got any horns, more's the pity! A smooth brow looks so ugly. I need one or two horns to give my sagging face a lift. Perhaps one will grow and I needn't be ashamed any more—then I could go and join them. But it will never grow! (*He looks at the palms of his hands.*) My hands are so limp—oh, why won't they get rough! (*He takes his coat off, undoes his shirt to look at his chest in the mirror.*) My skin is so slack. I can't stand this white, hairy body. Oh I'd love to have a hard skin in that wonderful dull green colour—a skin that looks decent naked without any hair on it, like theirs! (*He listens to the trumpetings.*) Their song is charming—a bit raucous perhaps, but it does have charm! I wish I could do it! (*He tries to imitate them.*) Ahh, Ahh, Brr! No, that's not it! Try again, louder! Ahh, Ahh, Brr! No, that's not it, it's too feeble, it's got no drive behind it. I'm not trumpeting at all; I'm just howling. Ahh, Ahh, Brr. There's a big difference between howling and trumpeting. I've only myself to blame; I should have gone with them while there was still time. Now it's too late! Now I'm a monster, just a monster. Now I'll never become a rhinoceros, never, never! I've gone past changing. I want to, I really do, but I can't, I just can't. I can't stand the sight of me. I'm too ashamed! (*He turns his back on the mirror.*) I'm so ugly! People who try to hang on to their individuality always come to a bad end!

We are dismayed to hear Berenger talking this way and seemingly on his way to join the herd. But we can recognize that Ionesco is telling us that to be human is also to want to fit into the group, to adjust to be accepted. Men do want both freedom and security; they want to hold the fort and fight on the frontier at the same time. There is a basic ambiguity in all of us. When Berenger finds that he cannot become a rhino, he suddenly snaps out of his self-pitying mood and shouts with defiance at the world gone mad:

Oh well, too bad! I'll take on the whole of them! I'll put up a fight against the lot of them, the whole lot of them! I'm the last man left, and I'm staying that way until the end. I'm not capitulating!

Berenger's final words do not deceive us. We know that he wants with all his heart to be a rhinoceros but cannot make it. He determines to make the best of a deteriorating situation. He fights for his individuality at the same time that he longs to be one of the herd. The recognition of this paradox within human nature helps us to understand some of the complexity of the human heart.

This same paradox is found in the religious life and in the Scriptures. The man of God is torn between his call to be a prophet and his preference for being a priest. A priest stands *with* the people. To be a prophet is to be an individual who stands *against* the crowd and calls them from idol worship to the adoration of the one true God. But the prophets bemoan their fate. Jeremiah wished he had never been born when he found himself beaten and imprisoned for speaking the word of Yahweh. How he would have liked to be one of the crowd, to say what the people wanted to hear, to enjoy the security of consensus, to be congratulated for his wisdom! Jeremiah really wanted to escape the responsibility of prophecy. But God had called him, and he could not escape his role.

Today there are "priests" who wish they could break away from their security and be "prophets" on the frontier; but the opportunity never comes to them. They are called to hold the fort, to guard the treasures of the past.

Ionesco is a secular "prophet." He is warning us that inauthentic existence, a bogus humanity, is appearing on earth as conformity creeps quietly over us. He reminds us that to succumb to this conformity is warm and comfortable, that it is not difficult to argue ourselves into the position that we want to be just like others and that the other-directed man, the organization man, is the handsomest of all. We are all under constant pressure to join the herd in our particular society. Ionesco challenges us to cry out with Berenger: "I'll put up a fight against the . . . lot of them! . . . I'm not capitulating!"

4
THE
LOSS OF INNOCENCE

THE BETTER MODERN MAN UNDERSTANDS HIMSELF, THE more clearly he realizes that he is guilty and dangerous. In our time, man has lost whatever was left of his sense of innocence and has become aware of the violence that hovers beneath the surface of his civilized rationality. This situation has fascinated the writers of our era, and they have delved into the theological doctrine of the fall of man in order to comprehend its symbolic meaning and to see its relevance today.

The late famous French novelist, Albert Camus, and a living American dramatist of note, Arthur Miller, have both produced works on this subject. Camus has given us *The Fall,* and Miller has provided *After the Fall.*

To begin, let us turn to the Biblical conception of the fall of Adam and see how it differs from the approach of the modern writers. In the Genesis narrative, man was created and placed in the Garden of Eden. He lived in a state of "dreaming innocence," in a paradise where he did not have to toil for a living, where there was no pain, illness, or death, where he was utterly secure—but without knowledge of good and evil. Adam and Eve disobeyed God by eating the forbidden fruit. Their eyes were opened; they knew the difference between good and evil. In that moment, man became a free, decision-making being; but he lost paradise. He lost his innocence and his harmlessness. Once driven out of the Garden of Eden, he could never return because an angel with a flaming sword guarded the entrance.

When we read the Biblical account, we feel that the Fall was a tragedy. Man lost his original happiness and became an earthbound, anxious, suffering, mortal being. If he had obeyed God and had left the forbidden fruit alone, he would still be enjoying Eden. In Christian theology, the first Adam lost Eden and separated himself from God; the Second Adam, Jesus Christ, overcame this separation and reconciled man with God. The crucifixion was the price Jesus had to pay to undo the sin of Adam.

To the modern writer, however, the Fall is not a tragedy, but a *victory* for man. Through the Fall, man became a human being, free to make decisions, aware of himself, able to rise out of his former submersion in animal nature. With the knowledge of good and evil came the appearance of conscience in mankind. The Fall is seen as the beginning of human history.

Without the Fall, man would have continued in a state of uncreative security. Through the Fall, man won freedom—and with it guilt, anxiety, and an awareness of his danger to other men and to himself.

ALBERT CAMUS / *The Fall*

Albert Camus, in *The Fall*, introduces us to a man who narrates the story of his life. His account is centered upon his recognition of the moment when he broke through from a false innocence into reality. He confesses himself to be a sinner, which means to him that all his life is self-centered. He cannot escape his self-will. He is in despair because, being a modern man, he does not possess faith and has no conception of grace or forgiveness. Toward the end of his story, he says to his listener:

> [Modern people] are free and hence have to shift for themselves; and since they don't want freedom or its judgments, they ask to be rapped on the knuckles, they invent dreadful rules, they rush out to build piles of faggots to replace churches. Savonarolas, I tell you. But they believe solely in sin, never in grace. They think of it, to be sure. Grace is what they want—acceptance, surrender, happiness.[25]

This fits with what Samuel Beckett is telling us in *Waiting for Godot*. Modern man is aware of waiting, but not of finding—or of being found. He knows of his sin, but nothing of the grace of God.

Camus has his narrator begin his tale by unfolding his early years when he was in "Eden." He was a young

[25] The quotations in this section on Camus are from *The Fall*, by Albert Camus, translated from the French by Justin O'Brien (Alfred A. Knopf, Inc.) © Alfred A. Knopf Inc., 1956. Used by permission of the publisher.

lawyer who believed himself to be a kindly, humble, generous, noble human being. "I was truly above reproach in my professional life. I never accepted a bribe, . . . never stooped either to any shady proceedings. . . . I never charged the poor a fee." He delighted in helping elderly and blind persons across the street and in giving alms to beggars. "I freely held sway bathed in a light as of Eden."

The lawyer, now a middle-aged man who has withdrawn from his profession, spends his time in barrooms, telling his story to selected listeners. The narrator is so accomplished a speaker that he is able to hold the attention of his listener, or victim, for several evenings.

He opens his "confession" by describing his one-time innocence. "Thus I progressed on the surface of life, in the realm of words as it were, never in reality." He relates how his virtuous security was badly shaken when, one night as he was especially conscious of a feeling of well-being, "I felt rising within me a vast feeling of power. . . . I straightened up and was about to light a cigarette, the cigarette of satisfaction, when, at that very moment, a laugh burst out behind me. Taken by surprise, I suddenly wheeled around; there was no one there."

He heard this laugh over and over. Always he looked for a person laughing, but could not find one. It became clear to him that the laugh was inside himself. It was the laugh of reality in the presence of his innocence.

His personal "fall" was completed one night when he was crossing a bridge on his way home. He saw a young woman standing by the railing gazing into the water. He walked on. When he was about fifty yards beyond the bridge, he heard the splash of a body striking the water and then a cry—

> I wanted to run and yet didn't stir. I was trembling, I believe from cold and shock. I told myself that I had to be quick and I felt an irresistible weakness steal over me. I have forgotten what I thought then. "Too late, too far . . ." or something of the sort. I was still listening as I stood motionless. Then, slowly under the rain, I went away. I informed no one.

Never again could he look upon himself as innocent. After this incident he became critical of all his actions and attitudes. He became acutely aware of "the fundamental duplicity of the human being. Then I realized . . . that modesty helped me to shine, humility to conquer, and virtue to oppress." He tried to forget what he had discovered about himself. He sought to escape into alcohol and promiscuity. They failed him, and he was left to face himself.

He became what Camus calls a "judge-penitent." He is both the accused and the judge. He is the sinner who whips himself with his sin. He never knows forgiveness, only the companionship of others who can be brought to recognize their own "fall." He tells his story to them in order to be a mirror for them and to induce them to tell their stories in turn.

When the narrator has completed his tale, he waits for his listener to confess—to prove that his portrayal is of everyman—by urging him on with the words,

"Then please tell me what happened to you one night on the quays of the Seine and how you managed never to risk your life."

Here Albert Camus leaves us. Man, when he faces reality, recognizes the loss of Eden. He is no longer secure, confident, and innocent. He is a person under judgment with no way to expiate the sin of being human. Camus has no answer for man's condition, only recognition and profound compassion.

ARTHUR MILLER/*After the Fall*

Arthur Miller also approaches the reality of life in terms of the Biblical account of the loss of Eden. His play, *After the Fall*, is in the form of a dramatized narration. The central character, as in Camus' novel, is a lawyer. His name is Quentin. In the play he is trying to understand himself, to recognize the sources of violence within his personality, to find out if he has anything left to offer to another human being in a close, personal relationship. There is a "Listener" in the first row of the audience to whom Quentin addresses his remarks. This listener could be a friend, a psychoanalyst, or even God. The author has suggested that he is Quentin, turned to look at himself. He never intrudes; he simply listens as the man pours out his story.

The play is an autobiography, presented in a series of memories or flashbacks. The stage setting consists of three levels. There are various pits and hollows, like lava, in the first two levels. Rising above them is the blasted stone tower of a German concentration camp. A dull grayness covers everything. Miller writes: "The action takes place in the mind, thought, and memory of Quentin. . . . The mind has no color, but its memories are brilliant against the grayness of its landscape." [26] The characters appear and disappear instantaneously, as in a dream. Lights pick them out and obliterate them when withdrawn. Quentin is surrounded by the human beings whose lives have touched and changed his.

Quentin tells us that he has quit his excellent job in a large law firm in New York City. He has lived through two divorces and several affairs. His disordered life has brought him to the edge of despair. He has met another woman, Holga, and is wondering if it would be possible for him to marry her. He is in an agony of indecision. He says to the Listener: "I don't know what I'd be bringing to that girl. I don't know what I believe about my own life!"

Quentin thinks back to his early days, when he was young and starting out in his profession. He saw things in black and white; he knew himself to be a noble young knight. He lived in his own Garden of Eden. He reminisces:

I look back to when there seemed to be a kind of plan, some duty in the sky. I had a dinner table and a wife, a child, and the world so wonderfully threat-

[26] This and the following quotations are from *After the Fall*, by Arthur Miller. Copyright © 1964 by Arthur Miller. All rights reserved. Reprinted by permission of The Viking Press, Inc. The text used here is from the version printed in *The Saturday Evening Post*, February, 1964.

ened by injustices I was born to correct! How fine!
Remember? When there were good people and bad
people? And how easy it was to tell! . . . When I
think of what I believed, I want to hide!

Then reality began to break in on him and he found
out that in life black and white are mixed and turn
into gray. He discovered that his marriage was not
working out as he had expected and that he was forced
to make a number of compromises in the course of his
daily legal work.

He hated to admit failure. When his first marriage
fell apart, he and his wife avoided the truth and lived
together for some years in dull misery. His wife finally
consulted a psychiatrist and found the courage to tell
him what was wrong in their relationship:

We don't seem . . . married. . . . You don't pay
any attention to me. . . . The way you behave toward me. I don't . . . *exist*. People are supposed to
find out about each other. I am not all this uninter-
esting, Quentin. Many people, men *and* women,
think I *am* interesting. . . . What am I to you? Do
you . . . do you ever *ask* me anything? Anything
personal? . . . You don't know me.

The marriage ended in divorce. Quentin was deeply
troubled by his inability to avoid this tragic break. His
troubles mounted because, as a liberal in politics, he had
been involved in activities that later were denounced
by a Senate committee as communist inspired. One of
Quentin's best friends was questioned by a Congressional
committee and named Quentin as one who had been a

member of a leftist group. He felt bewildered and betrayed. Many of his acquaintances turned against him and made him feel like a traitor.

During this period of turmoil, when he was feeling defeated and inadequate, he met Maggie, an open, affectionate, simple, beautiful young woman. When he met her she was the receptionist in his office and also a popular singer trying to win her way in her profession. Her life had been harsh and filled with many defeats. Quentin was attracted to her by the fact that she was not defending anything, upholding anything, or accusing. She was just *there,* and she accepted him without any questions. In his time of inadequacy and trial, he desperately needed someone to believe in him, to help him restore a sense of self-worth.

She was drawn to him because, as a man older than herself, he seemed so wise and because he seemed to find her valuable as a human being. In her experience, few men had taken her seriously; they had used her and turned away. Quentin told her she was honest and did not pretend to be innocent. He was delighted to find someone who would not club him to death with her innocence.

They were married. In the beginning, their life together was fully satisfying. He was masterful, she was dependent. But then her singing career began to develop successfully. She became a star in nightclubs and theaters. The acclaim of the public turned her head, and she became a narcissist, seeing only herself and seeking to further her career. She expected Quentin to wait upon her, to be her business manager, to submerge himself in her theatrical activities. She lost interest in him as a person and saw him as a part of her equipment. His own legal work began to suffer. The relationship between them deteriorated until a dark strangeness grew up in their marriage. He heard repeated the accusations of his first wife:

> MAGGIE: But Quentin . . . you should look at me more. I mean . . . like I *existed* or something. Like you used to look—out of your *self*. . . . Should never gotten married. . . . It all changes. Every man I ever knew they hate their wives.
> QUENTIN: Honey, it always comes down to the same thing, don't you see? Now listen to me. You're still proceeding on the basis that you're alone. That you can be disposed of. And the slightest contradiction of your wishes makes the earth tremble.

The marriage became a bitter conflict. Maggie drank a good deal and turned to sleeping pills for rest. Several times she had to be rushed to the hospital because of an overdose of drugs. Quentin tried to reach her, to help her face her problems and overcome them. He failed. He came to realize that Maggie and he were poison to each other. Then, one day, he left home for a while and had time to see his situation in perspective.

When he returned, he found Maggie in a haze of drink and drugs. He tried to explain what was going on between them:

> QUENTIN: Maggie, you want to die and I don't know anymore how to prevent it. Maybe it was just my

being out in the real world for twenty-four hours again, but it struck me that I'm playing with your life out of some idiotic hope of some kind that you're suddenly going to come out of this endless spell. I think somebody ought to be with you who has no illusions of that kind, and simply watches constantly to prevent it.

MAGGIE: Maybe a little love would prevent it.

QUENTIN: But how do you know, Maggie? Do you know who I am anymore? Aside from my name? I'm all the evil in the world, aren't I? All the betrayal, the broken hopes, the murderous revenge?

MAGGIE: And how'd that happen? Takes two to tango, kid. . . .

QUENTIN: A suicide kills two people, Maggie. That's what it's for. So I'm removing myself and perhaps it will lose its point. . . . You see what's happening? You've been setting me up for a murder.

Quentin's words were of no avail. Maggie was too deeply wounded by her life to be able to accept his insights, to embrace her own life and to live. She felt betrayed and destroyed by her husband. She accused him of never loving anyone but his daughter by his first wife. The conflict grew into a battle. Quentin tried to take the sleeping pills away from Maggie, and she fought him off. She told him she must have warmth and love, some "humanness." This made him recoil from her:

QUENTIN: . . . You are not going to kill me, Maggie, and that's all this is for!

MAGGIE: You liar!

QUENTIN: Not anymore—I am not guilty for your life! But I am responsible for my own. And I want those pills. I don't want to fight you, Maggie. Now put them in my hand.

As they struggled for the bottle of pills, Quentin suddenly lunged for Maggie's throat and began to strangle her, shouting: "You won't kill me! You won't kill me!" Suddenly realizing what he was doing, he released her in horror, with one word, "Murder?"

Maggie fell to the floor and looked up at him, *"her eyes victorious and wild with fear."* With great difficulty she spoke to him: "Now we both know. You tried to kill me, mister. I been killed by a lot of people, some couldn't hardly spell, but it's the same, mister. You're on the end of a long, long line, Frank."

Maggie collapsed. Quentin called the maid, and they sent for the ambulance and sent her to the hospital, where the doctors were able to save her life.

Then Quentin had to face himself and realize that he was capable of murder. In that instant his "innocence" left him forever. He had experienced the violence within himself, as within all mankind, and knew "that we are very dangerous!"

This seems to be the message that Arthur Miller wants to give to us today. The capacity to kill that is found in Quentin under provocation has also been demonstrated on a monstrous scale during the great wars of our era, and especially in the wanton execution of millions of Jews in Nazi Germany. The symbol of the blasted tower of the concentration camp on the stage in this play represents that larger violence in all mankind. Miller has Quentin say:

I am not alone, and no man lives who would not rather be the sole survivor of this place [the concentration camp] than all its finest victims! What is the cure! Who can be innocent again on this mountain of skulls! I tell you what I know! . . . My brothers died here . . . but my brothers built this place; our hearts have cut these stones!

For Miller, the fall of man, the expulsion from Eden, is the realization, "I know how to kill." It is the recognition "that we are very dangerous!" But this recognition is necessary for life to continue. The greatest threat to mankind, as Miller sees it, is an illusion of innocence. The innocent man or nation does not know of the existence of the violence within. Not knowing of this blind force, the man or nation will not guard against it and thus paves the way for a personal, or world, holocaust.

The only hope for mankind is to recognize that the Fall has taken place. Human aggression is a reality, no matter how deeply hidden within the individual or the people. We must be fully aware of it and constantly guard against it. Quentin finally says: "We meet unblessed; not in some garden of wax fruit and painted trees, that lie of Eden, but after, after the Fall, after many, many deaths. . . . And the wish to kill is never killed."

In the preface to his drama, Miller states his viewpoint in this way:

This play . . . is a way of looking at man and his human nature as the only source of the violence which has come closer and closer to destroying the race. It is a view which does not look toward social or political ideas as the creators of violence, but into the nature of the human being himself. It should be clear now that no people or political system has a monopoly on violence. It is also clear that the one common denominator in all violent acts is the human being.

We in America like to think of ourselves as an "innocent" nation. We recall our beginnings, how our ancestors departed from the evils of the old world and began a *new* society in this *new* world. The founders and pioneers thought that this society was peculiarly favored by the Almighty. Some even spoke of "God's American Israel." Over the years, this nation has grown strong and now possesses weapons that can destroy our entire civilization. There are always voices that call for the use of violence to gain our national goals. The other nations of the world pray that we will recognize how dangerous we are and, therefore, control our power.

In the personal story of the lawyer Quentin, we are told that this man was forced by the events of his life to face the truth about himself: that he is dangerous, a sinner. Only by facing this truth can he enter his own future and find compassion and forgiveness, for both himself and others. In a conversation between Quentin and the new woman he has met, we find recognized the theme of the acceptance that comes after the Fall:

> HOLGA: I had the same dream each night—that I had a child; and even in the dream I saw that the child was my life; and it was an idiot. And I wept, and a hundred times I ran away, but each time I came back it had the same dreadful face. Until I thought if I could kiss it, whatever in it was my own, perhaps I could rest. And I bent to its

broken face, and it was horrible. . . . But I kissed it.

QUENTIN: Does it still come back?

HOLGA: At times. But it somehow has the virtue now . . . of being mine. I think one must finally take one's life in one's arms, Quentin.

Through his harrowing experiences, Quentin comes to recognize his own egotism and cruelty; he comes to understand that he does not easily give himself to anyone. He becomes aware of others and their struggles, and learns pity. His "fall" is a tenderizing experience. But it is the beginning of mature, self-giving emotional life. Another way of describing the Fall is to say that it is the moment when one is able to embrace his own life.

The play closes with Quentin walking about amid the people of his life history.

> (*Now he arrives at Maggie; she rises from the floor webbed in with her demons, trying to awake. And with his life following him he climbs toward Holga, who raises her arm as though seeing him, and with great love . . .*)

HOLGA: Hello! (*He comes to a halt a few yards from her. A whispering goes up from all his people. He straightens against it and walks toward her holding out his hand.*)

QUENTIN: Hello. (*The darkness takes them all.*)

Arthur Miller in this play, and Albert Camus in his novel, have crossed beyond absurdity to compassion and courage. They speak about the fall of man, but not about the grace of God. Still, their work is a clear step beyond nihilism. It shows a new stirring of hope, an upsurge in the spirit of modern man.

5
DEATH
IN A SENSATE CULTURE

MODERN MAN IS AWARE OF HIS LONELINESS, HIS GUILT, his inner violence, and the absurdity of his life; but he is not aware of the grace or the forgiveness of God. His existence lacks any transcendent quality. He is earth-bound, but he is dissatisfied with this single dimension of his life. His situation is brought into sharp focus when he contemplates death.

Death is an experience that invades life from outside. Like birth, it is a mystery. Unlike "spiritual realities," death is not something that can be ignored. It really happens. No man escapes. It comes to the prince and the pauper, to the genius and the dullard. No human cunning can evade it; no great wealth can buy it off. Although men try to cover the abyss of absurdity in life with "togetherness," success, prestige, status, and the rest, they know that they cannot fool death.

Pitirim A. Sorokin, the late Harvard sociologist, has written that we live in a "sensate culture." By this he suggests that we accept as real only those things which we can perceive with our senses and with the extension of our senses in laboratory equipment. Extrasensory manifestations are denied serious consideration. We are a practical, sensible, hardheaded, scientific, no-nonsense generation. We work for tangible goals.

But what can a sensate culture make of death? It is the great contradiction. It reduces all sensate achievements to zero. It is the irrational threat that hovers over men in such a practical age.

Death becomes so threatening that the mention of it becomes obscene. In the Victorian era, sex was taboo and the discussion of sexual matters was considered pornographic. Today it is death that has become pornographic. In polite society it is *de rigueur* to talk about sex, especially if it is related to Freud and psychoanalysis, but it is forbidden to bring up the subject of death.

The lengths to which modern people will go to deny the reality of death are ridiculed in Evelyn Waugh's *The Loved One*. When death does take place, the mortician—never the "undertaker"—dresses the corpse and arranges its features to give the illusion of life. In some funeral "homes" the deceased is presented to "viewers" in a boudoir setting, the corpse dressed and reclining on a chaise longue. A "visit" takes place in which the visitors remark upon the naturalness of the body, "She might just be asleep." When it comes time for burial, the casket containing the body is placed in a watertight, airtight cement vault to preserve it from decay. All this and much more is done to evade the fact of death.

Time magazine presented an essay on death as it is

understood today. The author stated that a new approach to death is appearing in our time. "The rites of death and mourning . . . are growing more impersonal and grudging. Religiously, the promise of immortality has become dim and uncertain." [27] The concept of immortal life has no meaning in a sensate culture.

The essayist goes on to say that "modern man seems to be doing his best to dismiss death as an unfortunate incident." [28] Does this mean that our society is trying to delude itself into believing that death is some kind of hideous mistake? At all events, "dying is done offstage," in a hospital, usually, where the family and friends are not present for the last days and hours of suffering or drugged insensibility.

A dangerous result is that grief is going underground. Generally the request is that funerals be brief and without extended remarks or a eulogy. Black veils and widow's weeds have all but disappeared. Men seldom wear the black armband. Flowers are no longer hung on the door of the house to denote mourning within. All the conventional "grief work" of the past has been quietly abandoned. Even those close to the deceased are expected to carry on as before. This may be dangerous to us emotionally. Grief that goes underground is still grief and much stronger for being denied overt expression. As the *Time* essay suggests: "It may mean that we have to mourn covertly, by subterfuge—perhaps in various de-

[27] From "On Death as a Constant Companion," in *Time*, Nov. 12, 1965. © 1965 Time, Inc.
    [28] *Ibid.*

grees of depression, perhaps in mad flights of activity, perhaps in booze." [29]

Living in a sensate culture, man does not know how to handle this dark stranger from beyond. Death mocks all his pretenses of power and control of the universe. A final word from the *Time* essayist is most telling: "Alone with his elemental fear of death, modern man is especially troubled by the prospect of a meaningless death and a meaningless life." When death is meaningless, life becomes absurd. In his struggle for purpose, modern man will have to come to grips with the enigma of death.

TENNESSEE WILLIAMS / *The Milk Train Doesn't Stop Here Anymore*

Now let us turn to the contemporary dramatist, Tennessee Williams, and see how he deals with the threat of a meaningless death in his play, *The Milk Train Doesn't Stop Here Anymore*. Here we witness how a thoroughly sensate person faces her death and what happens to her "sense of life" as the moment grows closer.

In the drama we participate in the last two days in the life of Mrs. Flora Goforth, known to her few intimates as "Sissy." She lives in a spacious villa on a high hill overlooking the Mediterranean. At this point in her life she has achieved a splendid isolation from the world and from her former companions. She is surrounded by her servants, her bodyguard with his vicious dogs, and

[29] *Ibid.*

her secretary, Blackie. Mrs. Goforth is in late middle age
and is dying of cancer. She does not know of her condition, but feels sick in a variety of ways. She is engaged
in dictating her memoirs to her secretary.

A young man, Christopher Flanders, climbs the steep
hillside from the sea, fights off the watchdogs, and comes
to visit Sissy. He is a poet and a sculptor. He has made
it a practice to be with elderly persons and to help them
as they approach death. Because of this he is known to
the American colony in Italy as "the Angel of Death."

The name Christopher is symbolic. It means "Christ-
bearer." The nickname "the Angel of Death" indicates
that the older people in the colony around Rome feel
it is an ill omen when Christopher appears. Williams
seems to use Chris both as the messenger of death-at-
hand and as a kind of divine comforter. Chris says to the
secretary:

> Blackie, I've had a good bit of experience with old
> dying ladies, scared to death of dying, ladies with
> lives like Mrs. Goforth's behind them, which they
> won't think are over, and I've discovered it's possible
> to give them, at least to offer them, something closer
> to what they need than what they think they still
> want.[30]

Mrs. Goforth is both offended by his presence and
deeply glad to have him with her. With his assistance

[30] This quotation and those which follow are from *The Milk
Train Doesn't Stop Here Anymore*, by Tennessee Williams. Copyright © 1963, 1964 by Two Rivers Enterprises, Inc. Reprinted
by permission of the publisher, New Directions Publishing Corporation.

she is able to face the end of her life. The play closes as she dies.

Sissy Goforth is an excellent symbol for the modern individual conditioned by life in this sensate culture. A woman with a will of iron, she has had her way with everyone and everything she has met. She insists that she is in control of her life: "Sissy Goforth's not ready to go forth yet and won't go forth till she's ready." In talking with Christopher Flanders she speaks of herself as always a winner: "I give away nothing, I sell and I buy in my life, and I've always wound up with a profit, one way or another." We listen to her bravado and applaud her courage, but how does one wind up with a profit in the hour of death? How does one buy himself out of that inevitable event?

The panic that Mrs. Goforth feels beneath her brave words is revealed in her conversation with Blackie, when she says: "I've often wondered, but I've wondered *more* lately . . . meaning of *life*. Sometimes I think, I suspect, that everything that we do is a way of—*not* thinking about it. Meaning of life, and meaning of death, too . . . *What . . . are we doing?* Just going from one . . . frantic distraction to another, till finally one too many . . . frantic distractions leads to disaster, and blackout? Eclipse of, total of sun?" At another time she makes her panic even more specific: "Oh, God, Blackie, I'm *scared!* You know what I'm scared of? Possibly, maybe, the Boss is—dying this summer!"

With the exception of these glimpses of her panic, Sissy presents a tough face to the world. She admits nothing and seems to believe that her legendary existence will continue forever. Her life has been a struggle for recognition, luxury, wealth, pleasure, and domination. In middle life she is still a rapacious, spoiled child.

Sissy Goforth is the product of a sensate culture. She is a woman of driving vitality. She is a self-made person and is proud of it. As a striking and powerful personality, she has become well known in international society. Chris asks her how it feels to be a legend in her own lifetime. The question pleases her, and she tells him the story of her life:

> A legend in my own lifetime, yes, I reckon I am. Well, I had certain advantages, endowments to start with: a face people naturally noticed and a figure that was not just sensational, but very durable, too. . . . I was born between a swamp and the wrong side of the tracks in One Street, Georgia, but not even that could stop me in my tracks, wrong side or right side, or no side. Hit show-biz at fifteen when a carnival show, I mean the manager of it, saw me and dug me on that *one street* in One Street, Georgia. I was billed as the Dixie Doxy, was just supposed to move my anatomy, but was smart enough to keep my tongue moving, too, and the verbal comments I made on my anatomical motions while in motion were a public delight. So I breezed through show-biz like a tornado, rising from one-week "gigs" in the sticks to star billing in the Follies while still in m'teens, ho ho . . . and I was still in my teens when I married Harlon Goforth, a marriage into the Social Register and Dun and Bradstreet's, both. Was barely out of my teens when I became his widow. Scared to make out a will, he died intestate, so everything went to me.

Later, she married two other older, wealthy men who both died in turn and left her additional fortunes. Her fourth, and last, marriage was to a young, handsome man who, unfortunately, killed himself in an auto accident.

Christopher is much impressed by her strength of will and her ability to get what she wants. He has noticed that on her house flag is a picture of a griffin with gold wings. He tells Sissy that the mythological griffin represents "a force in life that's almost stronger than death."

Chris explains that his vocation is to care for another person. This gives him a sense of being sheltered, protected, from unreality and lostness. He says that human beings are like kittens or puppies in the house of their master. They play and romp in the daytime, but at night they huddle together for reassurance and protection. He continues to Sissy:

> We're all of us living in a house we're not used to . . . a house full of—voices, noises, objects, strange shadows, light that's even stranger— We can't understand. We bark and jump around and try to—be— *pleasingly playful* in this big mysterious house but— in our hearts we're all very frightened of it. Don't you think so? Then it gets to be dark. We're left alone with each other. We have to creep close to each other and give those gentle little nudges with our paws and our muzzles before we can slip into— sleep and—rest for the next day's—playtime . . . and the next day's mysteries.

It is this unreality and lostness, and "the next day's mysteries" that trouble man in a sensate culture. He refuses to think of himself as one who is not in complete

control. Sissy sees life as a battle: *"Grab, fight, or go
hungry!* Nothing else works."

Christopher patiently talks to the frightened self that
lies hidden behind the tough exterior of Sissy Goforth:

> May I tell you something about yourself? . . .
> You're suffering more than you need to. . . . You're
> suffering from the worst of all human maladies, of
> all afflictions, and I don't mean one of the body, I
> mean the thing people feel when they go from room
> to room for no reason, and then they go back from
> room to room for no reason, and then they go *out*
> for no reason and come back *in* for no reason—

He is speaking of the feeling of alienation and loneliness that is so common in modern life. A man fights his
way to success and affluence only to ask himself: "Is
this all? Is this what I gave all my years and my health
for?" When one nears death, this question becomes very
loud and insistent in one's mind.

It is difficult for us in a "practical" age to realize that
the act of living is also the process of dying. For, as
Chris expresses it, "We—all live in a house on fire, no fire
department to call; no way out, just the upstairs window
to look out of while the fire burns the house down with
us trapped, locked in it."

Sissy is upset by this morbid talk. She wants desperately to reassert herself and to get Chris in a situation
where she can dominate him. Her most successful
weapon in life has been her physical beauty. She uses
this to attempt to seduce him. He turns away from her.
"The Angel of Death" cannot be appeased by an appeal

to the senses. Chris tells her that he admires her vitality
and determination, but that her weapons will not help
her in the hours that lie ahead. He says: "You're nobody's fool, but you're a fool, Mrs. Goforth, if you don't
know that finally, sooner or later, you need somebody or
something to mean God to you, even if it's a cow on the
streets of Bombay, or carved rock on the Easter Islands."

She grasps, in part, what he is saying and asks if he
came to bring *God* to her: "Well, *bring* Him, I'm ready
to lay out a red carpet for Him, but how do you bring
Him? Whistle? Ring a bell for Him? (*She snatches a bell
off her desk and rings it fiercely.*) Huh? How? What?"

Chris knows that no one can bring God to another.
He is there to help Sissy get through her dying. He suggests that she learn the meaning of acceptance and stop
fighting for the impossible. Picking up the word "acceptance," she wants to know what she is to accept. He
answers:

> Oh, many things, everything, nearly. Such as how
> to live and to die in a way that's more dignified than
> most of us know how to do it. And of how not to be
> frightened of not knowing what isn't meant to be
> known, acceptance of not knowing *anything* but the
> moment of still existing, until we stop existing—and
> acceptance of that moment, too.

Sissy grows weaker. She is afraid and wants Chris to
leave her, to go on to his next appointment. She pulls
herself together and makes him a tough speech in her
old, dominating fashion:

Well, I've escorted four husbands to the eternal
threshold, and come back alone without them, just
with the loot of *three* of them, and, ah, . . . it was
like I was building a shell of bone round my heart
with their . . . loot, their loot the material for it—
It's my turn, now, to go forth, and I've got no choice
but to do it. But I'll do it alone. I don't want to be
escorted. I want to go forth alone. But you, you
counted on touching my heart because you'd heard
I was dying, and old dying people are your spe-
cialty, your vocation. But you miscalculated with
this one. This milk train doesn't stop here anymore.

She suggests that he go down to Naples and look for
another victim. But suddenly she becomes very weak and
asks him to help her to her bed, she can't make it alone.
He assists her to the bed and sits next to her. She begs
him, now, not to leave until— He assures her that he
never leaves until the end. She stretches out her hand to
him, he takes her hand. She whispers, "Be here, when I
wake up."

After Sissy's death, the secretary appears and asks if
the end was "peaceful." Chris nods, and the young
woman asks, "With all that fierce life in her?" Chris
answers: "You always wonder afterwards where it's gone,
so far, so quickly. You feel it must be still around somewhere, in the air. But there's no sign of it."

At the bottom of the steep hill is heard the breaking
of a wave. Chris says: *"Boom!"* Blackie asks him what
it means. The play ends with Chris replying: "It says
'Boom' and that's what it means. No translation, no ex-
planation, just 'Boom.'"

Tennessee Williams does not attempt to offer any religious consolation at the moment of death. He lets us witness the struggle of a woman of great vitality, a true member of our sensate culture, as death closes in. The author understands this woman and has compassion for her. Through his characters he himself struggles with the problem of death in our time. He acknowledges the mystery of life and death. He makes it clear that people facing these mysteries need "something" to mean God to them, for human strength is not enough to carry one through. Williams comes up with no Christian answer, but with a Stoic conception of resignation to the facts of our human existence.

To provide a true mirror for our culture, a dramatist could hardly go farther than Williams has gone. This is a post-Christian age, and people live and die without a belief in the resurrection or the continuing concern of God for them in both life and death. The apostle Paul's belief that there is nothing in life or death that can separate us from the love of God in Christ Jesus is foreign to our modern existence.

It is important for us to know how our generation sees life and death. We live at a time that is very much like the world of the first century, with its Stoicism, Epicureanism, leader worship, and mystery cults. Although it is a post-Christian age, it is also, in a way, a *pre*-Christian age. The New Testament message that in Christ death is swallowed up in victory, that death has lost its sting, that faith in Christ is freedom from sin and death—this is *the* message which the modern world wants so much to hear, but it has not yet heard.

In a sensate culture, man's sense of reality is limited

by what he can see, hear, taste, touch, or experience
emotionally. Ideas and concepts are somewhat real but
are also suspect. Life is practical; and worldly goals of
success, prestige, power, happiness, are the only real
goals.

The man of faith, however, has a different sense of
reality. He sees the physical things of the world and yet
is aware of realities that transcend that world. He has
knowledge of grace, forgiveness, eternal life. His reality
is bounded not by the world but by eternity, the realm
of God. The sense of reality in modern cultures clashes
with the Christian sense of reality, and a conflict is established that makes it difficult for the practical man of
our era to take the Christian faith seriously.

Tennessee Williams is aware of this conflict and has
Chris speak of it to Sissy Goforth:

> We don't all live in the same world, you know,
> Mrs. Goforth. Oh, we all see the same things—sea,
> sun, sky, human faces and inhuman faces, but—
> they're different in *here!* (*Touches his forehead.*)
> And one person's sense of reality can be another
> person's sense of—well, of madness!—chaos!— . . .
> When one person's sense of reality seems too—
> disturbingly different from another person's . . .
> [sense of reality] . . . Well, he's—avoided! Not
> welcome! It's—*that simple.* . . . And—yesterday in
> Naples, I suddenly realized that I was in that situa-
> tion. I found out that I was now a—*leper!* . . .
> They hang labels, tags of false identification, on
> people that disturb their own sense of reality too
> much, like the bells that used to be hung on the
> necks of—lepers!

In a sensate culture with its world-centered philosophy, Christians often feel like lepers. Their transcendent sense of reality disturbs the practical world. Mrs. Goforth tried to be rid of Christopher, the Christ-bearer, but in the end she knew his sense of reality was more important than hers: "Be here, when I wake up."

EUGÈNE IONESCO/*Exit the King*

Another view of death in our culture is provided by Eugène Ionesco, that Romanian dramatist who has lived and worked in Paris for many years, in his play *Exit the King*. Modern man, conditioned to living in a sensate society, sees himself as the ruler of his personal existence. During the time that we are at the height of our life, we are monarchs of our little realms. When we are healthy and strong, our bodies obey us and we seem to have a number of devoted, obedient servants. But when the process of aging begins, our "servants" no longer obey and our kingdom begins to crumble. The latter part of life, as death approaches, is like the experience of a king who is losing his power and whose kingdom is falling apart.

This viewpoint is regularly avoided by modern people who prefer to think only in terms of life and human strength. Writing on this subject in *Holiday* magazine, Alan Brien makes the observation: "If we really thought, as our forebears did, that each day was numbered and nontransferable, would so many of us still carry on with graceless, pointless, monotonous jobs, which give us so

little pleasure and are of so little advantage to our
neighbors? Are we not sustained by the progressive illusion, patented in this century, that when we stop working
for a living we will inherit a golden, adult Disneyland of
dignified leisure and high-minded tranquillity where we
will live for a living through all time?"

The highly touted American retirement community is
never presented as a place for those in the declining
years as powers diminish; it is advertised as an environment filled with fellowship, creative activity, and enjoyable recreation. Retirement is seen as a period in life
when hopes can be fulfilled as the drudgery of work is
left behind. This is an illusion "patented in this century."
The high point of modern man's life is not in his career
but in his retirement.

To those who accept this illusion, the experience of
actual retirement comes as a rude awakening. We may
try to keep death hidden from ourselves, but it makes
itself known in subtle ways as our powers dwindle. The
Biblical concept of death as a part of life and the experience of our ancestors that in the midst of life we are in
the midst of death is strange to the thinking of men and
women in our time. As Alan Brien says: "At last, I begin
to see that the candid acceptance of the universality and
inevitability of death is a revolutionary, not a conservative, impulse."

We might say that this discovery of the inevitability
of death is not so much revolutionary as it is a startling
renewed awareness of a truth hidden deep in our consciousness. When events bring this awareness to the sur-

face, we have the pathetic situation of a human being unprepared for the inevitable. A newspaper reports these words of an elderly person: "I am an old man and I am afraid to die. How can I get rid of this awful dread of death?" What can we say to such a man? In a culture that tried to banish the very thought of death, that considered death an obscenity, how is the individual prepared for his last years and his inevitable demise?

Eugène Ionesco wrote his play in order to come to terms with this strange phenomenon in our society. He, himself, is vividly aware of his own coming death. In London, after the great success of his tragicomedy, *Rhinoceros,* a critic met Mrs. Ionesco and suggested that her husband must be happy over the triumph of his masterpiece. She replied that, on the contrary, he was sad. In surprise, the critic asked why this was so and she answered: "He is afraid of death." Obviously, this awareness of death hovers over all his moments of success. This is the hidden knowledge of all men, even in a sensate age. Ionesco the artist is able to delve into the substratum of human existence and to draw out of it the obsessions that torment all of us. In his plays, our private nightmares appear onstage and we realize that we are all members of one family. It is, as Alan Brien points out, "oddly comforting to realize that everyone, but everyone, is in the same boat."

Death has a different meaning for us than it had for people in former ages. Medieval man lived always in the presence of death. It often came to him through plague or accident in the midst of life. Modern scientific medi-

cine has added many years to our lives. In the United
States, 10 percent of our population is over sixty-five
years old today. That means over twenty million persons.
A century ago, only 2.5 percent of Americans were over
sixty-five. With an increasing number of persons living
longer, the concept of death is changing from a sudden
surprise to a prolonged process of disintegration. This
presents modern man with a new set of facts with which
to deal in his declining years.

Walter Kerr, the drama critic of *The New York Times*,
has written about *Exit the King:* "The play has to do
with the coming of Death, exactly as *Everyman* (the
medieval morality play) does; it is, in fact, nothing more
than *Everyman* rewritten by a twentieth-century sensibility. But that sensibility experiences disillusion very
differently from the writer, or the hero, of a medieval
allegory. In fact, in the original *Everyman* the victim
does not experience disillusion at all. Death comes for
him—sliding a dark black hand over his heart while he
chats at a banquet—and whisks him bodily and whole, to
heaven or hell, from a world that remains whole behind
him. Nothing is dissolved or ended. The man is simply
taken out of the world. In *Exit the King* exactly the opposite happens. The world is taken out of the man."

When we visit with elderly individuals in our society,
we become acutely aware of the fact that the world is
disappearing around them. Their interests narrow, their
view of existence is constricted, they tend to dwell upon
the familiar and, very often, the distant past that is well
known to them. It is this experience that Ionesco seeks

to express in his play. Each of us is the monarch of his own consciousness. Each one's world is a product of his own perceptions or awareness. As we grow old, our world contracts and our control over our kingdom lessens. It seems as if the world withdraws from us until, finally, we are isolated and powerless.

The setting for *Exit the King* is the throne room in a once well appointed royal castle. The room is now vaguely dilapidated. Cracks are appearing in the walls. The decorations need renewing or replacement. The throne is at the back of the stage with steps leading up to it. On either side are smaller thrones for the two queens.

As befits the subject matter, the cast is restricted to the king, Berenger the First; his older wife, Queen Marguerite; his younger wife, Queen Marie; the Doctor, who also appears as the Surgeon, Executioner, Bacteriologist, and Astrologer; a woman, Juliette, who is both Domestic Help and Registered Nurse; and a Guard. We never see the rest of his retinue or any of the other members of his realm.

The signs of dissolution are evident. The heating system no longer functions. The army does not even pretend to be defending the kingdom. Citizens are leaving for other countries. But King Berenger has been so taken up with entertaining his younger queen that he has not noticed what has been happening. Marie has been content to join him in his distractions and has not made any attempt to prepare him for what is ahead. The older Queen Marguerite is more practical, and she upbraids

Marie: "It's your fault if he's not prepared. It's your fault if it takes him by surprise. You let him go his own way. You've even led him astray. Oh yes! Life was very sweet. With your fun and games, your dances, your processions, your official dinners, your winning ways and your fireworks displays, your silver spoons and your honeymoons!" [31] Marguerite feels that it is her duty to help the king understand the reality of his situation. She says severely: "He should have his eyes fixed in front of him, know every stage in the journey, know exactly how long the road, and never lose sight of his destination."

Marguerite wants the king to face the facts. She states them baldly: "His palace is crumbling. His fields lie fallow. His mountains are sinking. The sea has broken the dikes and flooded the country. He's let it all go to rack and ruin." When Marie claims that Berenger is still young, Marguerite answers that he *was* young yesterday, or even last night, but that it is no longer true.

When we look back, events in life seem to rush together. Time speeds up in our memories and childhood seems but yesterday. As the Doctor observes: "Yesterday evening it was spring. It left us two hours and thirty minutes ago. Now it's November." An aging person carries within himself all the stages of his life and they tend to intermingle. He is surprised when he looks in the mirror and finds himself an old man. Where have the years gone? Yesterday evening it *was* spring!

[31] This quotation and those which follow are from *Exit the King*, by Eugène Ionesco, translated from the French by Donald Watson (Grove Press, Inc.). Copyright © 1963 by John Calder (Publishers), Ltd. Used by permission of Grove Press, Inc.

King Berenger appears and complains bitterly about his aches and pains. His legs are stiff, his feet hurt, he has a touch of lumbago, and he has not slept well. He peers at the Doctor and his two queens and says: "Why are you staring at me like this? Is there something abnormal about me? Now it's so normal to be abnormal, there's no such thing as abnormality. So that's straightened that out."

Queen Marguerite decides to tell the king the truth. Marie tries to stop her but she brushes the younger queen aside and states the fact to the king that he is going to die. The king sweeps the news aside, saying that he knows all about it, that we all do, and suggesting that Marguerite remind him of it when the time comes. The Doctor interrupts to point out that the older queen is right; he *is* going to die. This irritates Berenger who answers in a very human way: "What, again? You get on my nerves! I'll die, yes, I'll die all right. In forty, fifty, three hundred years. Or even later. When I want to, when I've got the time, when I make up my mind. Meanwhile, let's get on with affairs of state. (*He climbs the steps of the throne.*) Ouch! My legs! My back! I've caught a cold. . . . This throne's got very hard!"

It is almost impossible for a human being to take seriously his own death. Like the king, we admit that death is a fact but we put it off into the future, the distant future. It becomes a kind of disagreeable illusion. The signs of disintegration are in the king's body and around him in his kingdom that is ceasing to function bit by bit, but the king prefers not to take them

seriously. He insists he will find remedies. He will re-
new his kingdom. He will recover from his personal ail-
ments.

The Doctor tells him quietly that he is now incurable.
The king counters by saying that he feels fine. Marguerite startles him by stating that he will die in an hour
and a half, at the end of the show. The king insists that
he is in charge and that no one can give such orders
without his consent: "I'll die when I want to. I'm the
king. I'm the one to decide." But the Doctor replies that,
even though he is king, he has lost the power to decide
this final issue.

The king is angered and orders the Guard to arrest
Marguerite and the Doctor as traitors. But the Guard
finds he cannot move. He cannot obey the king. Marie
urges the king on and insists that he can rule by will
power. Marie and the Guard cry out: "Long live the
King!" but the older queen remarks: "What a farce!"

Marie declares that she will obey the king and asks
him to give a command. It is her belief that love can
overcome all things, even death. Her love for the king
will give him back his power. He is grateful for her confidence in him and orders her to approach the throne.
Marie finds she cannot move. Tearfully, she begs: "Forgive me, your Majesty. It's not my fault."

It begins to dawn upon Berenger that he is no longer
the all-powerful monarch, that his commands are not
going to be obeyed, that he is, indeed, going to die. This
terrifies him. He cannot abide the thought. He pleads
with the others: "I don't want to die. Please don't let me

die! Be kind to me, all of you, don't let me die! I don't want to." The Doctor calls this the first crisis in dying. It is perfectly normal. The question is, Can the king be led through the crisis into an acceptance of his passing? Can he be helped to find the dignity necessary to face his death in a royal manner?

Marguerite and the Doctor point out to Berenger that he did not prepare himself for this moment. He let the years go by without thinking seriously about his own death. He had perfunctory thoughts on the matter, but he never faced it with all his heart and soul. He pushed the truth away from himself and, with the help of sycophants in his court and the distractions of his young queen, he was able to banish the concept of death and to treat it as an illusion. "He never looked ahead, he's always lived from day to day, like most people."

This attitude is found in our entire modern society. We have tried to sweep the thought of death aside. It is our form of pornography. It is not mentioned in polite society. Our dying is done "offstage" in hospitals and nursing homes. In John Galsworthy's *Forsythe Saga* when an older member of the family is dying, an elaborate deathbed scene is played out. The relatives gather. The last words and instructions are heard with earnestness and taken seriously. The individual leaves this world with dignity. This Victorian style in dying has been superseded in our day. We pretend that death does not happen. We refuse to prepare for it. Death, therefore, takes modern men unawares and they play the scene badly. Like Berenger, they plead for more time and die in an agony of unpreparedness. Or they are drugged and drift away without knowing what is taking place. Berenger, in the play, bewails his lack of preparation: "I'm like a schoolboy who hasn't done his homework and sits for an exam without swatting up the papers . . . like an actor on the first night who doesn't know his lines and who dries, dries, dries. Like an orator pushed onto a platform who's forgotten his speech and has no idea who he's meant to be addressing. I don't know this audience, and I don't want to. I've nothing to say to them. What a state I'm in!"

While the king is quite beside himself with anxiety over his condition, the Doctor reminds him that it is his duty as a king to die with dignity. But Berenger insists: "It's impossible. I'm frightened. It's impossible." In reply to this, Marguerite declares flatly: "He imagines no one's ever died before." This is quite a common human reaction. Our own death is always unique. It *is* difficult to believe that it ever happened to anyone else in quite the same way. The death of another is an incident in our lives; our own death is the collapse of our whole world. Thus, in a sense, no one else has ever died.

The king cries out for help from his people, but no one answers. He wants to go for a walk, but he finds himself staggering. He screams in frustration. His hair has turned white. They take his scepter and his crown from him; they are too heavy. He insists they return his scepter. He hopes it is all a dream, a nightmare. He tells them all to be silent. Then he begs them to talk to him. He cries out in anguish: "Why was I born if it wasn't forever?

Damn my parents! What a joke, what a farce! I came into the world five minutes ago. I got married three minutes ago. . . . Never had time to get to know life. . . . I never had the time, I never had the time, I never had the time!"

As the truth bears in upon him, the king begins to realize that he is not above the law; he is just like everybody else. But then he begins to think about living on in the memory of his people. He wants to control the future when he is not present: "Oh, please make them all remember me! Make them weep and despair and perpetuate my memory in all their history books. Make everyone learn my life by heart. Make them all live it again. Let the schoolchildren and the scholars study nothing else but me, my kingdom and my exploits. . . . Let my likeness be on all the ikons."

This is a common longing for all of us. Wealthy men draw up their wills in such a way that they can control how their money will be spent for several generations. They cannot bear to think of a world without them. They seek to extend their power. The most humble of men wants to be remembered. Ionesco seems to be saying that this is a stage through which one must pass in the process of dying. We can accept our own demise if we can imagine that we shall be remembered. It is a way of softening the blow.

But this respite is brief. The king becomes aware that in death his body will become a corpse. The Doctor offers to see that the body is embalmed and preserved. This thought horrifies Berenger: "I don't want to be embalmed. I want nothing to do with that corpse. I don't want to be burnt. I don't want to be buried, I don't want to be thrown to the wild beasts or the vultures. I want to feel arms around me, warm arms, cool arms, soft arms, strong arms."

We mortals cannot easily separate ourselves from our bodies. We have lived in them too long. They are precious to us. In death, we want to be treated as in life. The king turns for comfort to his younger queen who tries to calm him with brave illusions about living for the "now" and forgetting such words as "exist" and "die." She tells him that if he can escape from definitions, he will be free again and will be able to breathe. She tries to weave a spell: "Open the floodgates of joy and light to dazzle and confound you. Illuminating waves of joy will fill your veins with wonder. If you want them to."

These words are ineffectual. The king is beyond such "inspiration" and coddling. Muttering to himself, he searches for some kind of assistance: "Help me, you countless thousands who died before me! Tell me how you managed to accept death and die. Then teach me! . . . Assist me, you who were frightened and did not want to go! What was it like? . . . Were you afraid to the very end? And you who were strong and courageous, who accepted death with indifference and serenity, teach me your indifference and serenity, teach me resignation!"

The Doctor suggests that he might provide euphoric pills or tranquilizers, but Marguerite insists that the king must learn how to let go and surrender completely. Marie admits she cannot help him anymore. The king is staggering about the throne room. He falls several times and drags himself to his feet again. He keeps reminding himself that he is still aware of things and people. He seems to be fading away when he suddenly tries another tack and attempts to interest himself in the life of Juliette, the Domestic and Registered Nurse. He asks her if she has mended his clothes. He asks her what she thinks about and what her husband does. He begs her to talk to him. He finds that he knows nothing about her as a person, though she has been in the castle for many years. She tells him she is a widow and lives a very hard life. Berenger thinks about this and says that life can never be bad. He sees that as a contradiction in terms. Juliette tells him of her many problems. Doing the royal laundry hurts her hands and cracks her skin. Making beds, polishing the floors, sweeping, give her the backache and a pain in the kidneys. The king thinks wonderingly about the fact we all have backs and kidneys and that pain is, at least, a sign of life. She says that she has to dig in the garden and that her constant drudgery makes her exhausted. He declares that she should have told him her troubles. Juliette answers that she did, but he never noticed or heard her. He still does not hear her. All he can think of is the continuing of life for her, with all its burdens and hardships. His seeming concern for her was actually his attempt to keep his mind off his coming death. "He wants to gain time," says the Doctor.

In conversation with Juliette, he is reminded that she is the cook. Berenger remembers all the things he likes to eat—stew, potatoes, carrots, gravy. He realizes that he must give them up. When one's kingdom disintegrates, the minor cravings go first. The king is beginning to understand what is happening to him. He is still in a cold sweat, but he is no longer fighting the process of dying. The Doctor observes: "He's not used to being so terrified yet, oh no! But now he can see the fear inside him; that's why he's dared to close his eyes. He'll open them again. He still looks tense, but see how the wrinkles of old age are settling on his face. Already he's letting things take their course. He'll still have a few setbacks. It's not as quick as all that. But he won't have the wind up anymore. That would have been too degrading. He'll still be subject to fright, but pure fright, without abdominal complications. We can't hope this death will be an example to others. But it will be fairly respectable. His *death* will kill him now, and not his fear."

Marie tries to call him back by reminding him of her love for him. Berenger looks at her wearily and tells her that it doesn't seem to help. Marie tries to interest him in the new discoveries of science, the expansion of knowledge, but the king can only repeat the self-centered words: "I'm dying." What is happening outside of himself no longer matters. His interest has narrowed to the fact that he is dying. There seems to be no way to reach him. Marie tries desperately to gain his attention, to remind him of their former happy life together; but he looks at Marguerite and says: "I don't know you, I don't love you."

The king's vision blurs. He is going blind. The walls of the throne room seem to disappear. People suddenly disappear, one after the other, Marie, the Guard, Juliette, the Doctor. Only Marguerite is left with Berenger. He wants to call back the others. But he cannot remember their names. Marguerite seeks to help him by cutting away from him all the possessions that tie him down . . . "an odd collection of bits and pieces, horrid things that live on you like parasites. . . . You're sagging under the load, your shoulders are bent, that's what makes you feel so old. (*She frees him of the invisible weight.*) That's better! How did you manage to trail them around all your life?"

It is difficult to persuade the king to give up his possessions. He is floundering. He can only stammer the word, "Me." The older queen remarks: "He imagines he's *everything!* He thinks *his* existence is *all* existence." She proceeds to try to drive that idea out of his mind. He loses the ability to speak. Marguerite helps him to walk toward his throne and insists that he climb the few steps up to his regal seat. He sits there unseeing and motionless, like a statue. She commands him to give her his fingers, his arms, his chest, his shoulders, his stomach. She says: "There you are, you see! Now you've lost the power of speech, there's no need for your heart to beat, no more need to breathe. It was a lot of fuss about nothing, wasn't it?"

Suddenly, Queen Marguerite disappears. The king is left alone, seated on his throne. The doors, windows, and walls of the room have faded away. A grayish lights fills the stage. Slowly the king and the throne melt away and there is nothing but the gray light.

Eugène Ionesco knows from personal experience what it means to be afraid of death. In *Exit the King*, he has attempted to express his emotional responses in terms of a king whose kingdom has disintegrated around him. It is a telling allegory. Each of us is a king of his own consciousness and the coming of death to a human being is the process of the narrowing of that consciousness until only a flicker of self-awareness remains. Ionesco uses this parable to reveal how death comes to all men.

The younger queen, Marie, tries to shield Berenger from what is happening to him by suggesting various illusions. By speaking of her human love for the king and his powers as a monarch, she hopes to banish his fear of death which, she insists, is not real or final. But the king is not taken in. As the process of disintegration continues, he slowly comes to terms with it. His panic gives way to resignation. Death *is* real and it brings an end to earthly life. There is no "immortal" element in human personality that passes through death.

The Christian faith has always known this fact. It is a resurrection faith. The center of the gospel is a witness to the resurrection. This is the burden of the first Christian sermons reported in the book of The Acts. The resurrection has meaning only if death is real and final, and Christians affirm that God raised Christ from the dead. In Christ, all believers receive this gift of new life.

Men are forced to face the absurdity and finality of death in order to be open to the gift of new life in Christ. In the New Testament, death is overcome by the power of God, not by any immortal quality in man. Because we live in a secular age, in a sensate culture, death has become the final enemy. If we remove the message of the resurrection and a deep human response to it, then human beings are left to face death as the final dissolution. Then the only weapon is illusion.

Ionesco is a brave man. He is willing to face the absurdity of death, to follow its disintegrating process, to ask us to go on this terrifying journey with him. We must take him seriously and realize that he fashions for us a fitting prelude to the gospel. The Christian message is powerful only as it comes to terms with the exit of kings . . . remembering that each of us is a king in his own particular realm.

Tennessee Williams and Eugène Ionesco enable us to comprehend how our contemporaries understand death. Both playwrights have dug down into the modern human subconscious and have faced the obsessions, fears, and neuroses hidden there. Our society tries to hide its reactions to death which is so threatening. But when we are forced to face that which terrifies, we find it can be a liberating and exhilarating experience. We realize that our private panic is common to all persons. It also makes us ready to join that other community where faith in a God who gives new life, who is the Lord of resurrection, informs human consciousness.

6
THE ABSTRACT
AND THE CONCRETE

EDWARD ALBEE IS A YOUNG AMERICAN PLAYWRIGHT WHO is making a tremendous impact upon the theater in this country and abroad. His reputation rests, in the main, on four plays: *The Zoo Story, The American Dream, Who's Afraid of Virginia Woolf?* and *Tiny Alice.* He acts as both mirror and critic of the American way of life.

If we want to communicate with people in our culture today, it is important for us to listen to a man like Albee. He knows by instinct, experience, and study the questions modern men and women are asking. He knows their difficulty in trying to find an identity in a time of technological facelessness. He knows what it is to be alone in a vast crowd, to feel abandoned, to be betrayed. He knows how it is when illusions are smashed, and one is forced to stare into the emptiness of an absurd reality. He knows how to feel compassion for his neighbors who are caught in these bewildering problems.

Albee has thought of himself in a kind of prophetic role. In talking to John Gielgud, the British actor who played the leading role on Broadway in *Tiny Alice,* Albee said, "I've always thought that it was one of the responsibilities of playwrights to show people how they are and what their time is like in the hope that perhaps they'll change it." [32]

Three elements in this statement need to be noted: (1) he hopes to show people *how they are* (the "mirror" function); (2) he wants to help people understand *what their time is like* (the sociological function); and (3) he does these two things in the hope that *perhaps they'll change it* (the moral function). Albee possesses a sense of responsibility toward people and toward our society. He hopes for a better world—where individuals know who they are, relate successfully to one another, live together in peace, and have a sense of ultimate security.

Albee has caught the spirit of this "open" period in history in which we live. As the atomic physicists have broken out of the "box" of classical physics into a new realm of mystery, so Edward Albee has broken away from the traditional views of our culture and is on the frontier of a changing era.

He finds himself in a difficult position because the average man does not like to follow him out to the frontier. As Albee said to Gielgud, "The basic crisis the theater's in now is that the audience primarily wants a reaffirmation of its values, wants to see the *status quo,* wants to

[32] From "John Gielgud and Edward Albee Talk About the Theater," by R. S. Stewart, in *Atlantic,* April, 1965. Copyright © 1965 by The Alantic Monthly Company.

be entertained rather than disturbed, wants to be comforted and really doesn't want any kind of adventure in the theater." [33]

EDWARD ALBEE/*Tiny Alice*

In this play, *Tiny Alice,* Albee is concerned with the abstract and the concrete in human experience. He has called this drama "an examination of how much false illusion we need in order to get through life; also the difference between the abstraction of God and the God we make in our own image." [34]

The plot of the drama is uncomplicated, although the interpretation of the actions and words is difficult. The play opens with a conversation between a cardinal and a lawyer about an offer by Miss Alice, the richest woman in the world, to give the Roman Catholic Church a hundred million dollars a year for the next twenty years. It is stipulated that a lay brother, Julian, who is secretary to the Cardinal, shall make the proper arrangements.

In the next scene, Julian arrives at Miss Alice's castle and meets the Lawyer and the Butler. These are strange characters whose functions seem to reach far beyond their status as adviser and servant to Miss Alice. We have the feeling that the three make up a triumvirate in conspiracy.

Julian is persuaded to take up residence in the castle

[33] *Ibid.*

[34] Quoted by Jerry Tallmer in an interview with Edward Albee, *New York Post,* March 23, 1966. © 1966 New York Post Corporation.

in order to make sure that the generous gift flows smoothly into the coffers of the church. He becomes friendly with Miss Alice and shares his personal hopes and fears with her. They seem to fall in love; at least, Julian loves her. Miss Alice seduces him. They plan to be married, and the Cardinal comes to perform the wedding ceremony.

After the wedding, Julian expects to go away with his bride; but he is told by the Lawyer that he is to remain in the castle while the rest leave. The Cardinal departs with a large installment of the gift in a suitcase. When Julian refuses to remain alone and demands that his bride, Miss Alice, stay with him, he is shot and mortally wounded by the Lawyer. All leave, and Julian dies in agony, crying out for Alice and for God. In his agony, however, there is also the intimation of ecstasy in martyrdom.

A central element in the castle scene is a huge dollhouse model of the castle, an exact replica of the larger building. What is more strange is that whatever takes place in the castle also takes place in the model. Lights go on and off in the model as people move around in the castle. When the chapel in the model suddenly begins to smoke, it is discovered that the chapel in the castle has caught fire. Thus the model mirrors what happens in the castle.

This is not all. When Julian is inspecting the model, the Butler asks him if he has noticed that there is a model within the model and suggests, "You don't suppose that within that tiny model in the model there, there is . . .

another room like this, with yet a tinier model within it, and within . . ." [35]

As the play continues, one receives the impression that the symbolism of the model goes both ways, that the stage within the theater is a model within a larger model within a yet larger model—and so on to infinity. This is the feeling we have as we live today in a universe that seems to expand in two directions. Our world is within a universe that is within a larger universe. And the atom has turned out to be a miniature universe with smaller universes within. Man can look out and in; he can use both a telescope and a microscope to look toward infinity.

In the play, the lawyer has made an investigation of the life of Brother Julian. He knows everything about him, except for six "hidden" years. He is naturally curious about them, but Julian will not enlighten him. With the Butler and Miss Alice, however, it is a different matter, and Julian is willing to disclose to them what took place. To the Butler he explains:

> I . . . I lost my faith. (*Pause*) In God. . . . I . . . declined. . . . I . . . shriveled into myself; a glass dome . . . descended, and it seemed I was out of reach, unreachable, finally unreaching, in this . . . paralysis, of sorts. I . . . put myself in a mental home. . . . I could not reconcile myself to the chasm between the nature of God and the use to which men put . . . God.

The Butler asks if he means that he cannot stand the difference between his God and others', between his view of God and theirs. Julian replies: "I said what I intended: It is God the mover, not God the puppet; God the creator, not the God created by man. . . . Men create a false God in their own image, it is easier for them!"

To Miss Alice, Julian says, "Man's God and mine are not . . . close friends." He explains that he lost his faith because of the way people mock God. "I was confused . . . *and* intimidated . . . by the world about me, and let slip contact with it . . . with my faith."

Julian, the lay brother who never felt worthy to become a priest, seeks the "God beyond God," as Paul Tillich used to put it. Julian longs to know the God who is beyond the symbols of the church and the explanations of the theologians. Although a faithful son of the church, he struggles against accepting what the church tells him about God.

In the drama, Albee seems to be testing Julian's faith in a God whose reality lies beyond all concrete symbols, including the symbols of language. Can he be persuaded to accept a symbol for the reality, the concrete for the abstract? This is the question Albee raises in *Tiny Alice*.

The Lawyer, the Butler, and Miss Alice conspire to detach Julian from concrete reality and leave him with the abstract, which is called "Alice" to distinguish it (her? him?) from *Miss* Alice. At various times we hear Miss Alice praying to "Alice," making it clear that this abstract being is in charge of what is happening onstage.

The conspiracy comes into focus when the Butler asks the Lawyer: "Isn't a hundred million a year for twenty years enough? For one man? He's not even a priest." Later, the Lawyer turns to the model of the castle and speaks to "Alice": "Rest easy; you'll have him. . . . You will have your Julian. Wait for him. He will be yours."

When Julian is seduced by Miss Alice, she is acting for "Alice." She says to him: "Alice says she wants you, come to Alice, Alice tells me so, she wants you, come to Alice . . . Alice! . . . Alice? . . . He will be yours! He will be yours! AAAALLLLIIIICCCCEEEE!" The last part of this speech points to the offering of a sacrifice by Miss Alice to the abstract being.

When the marriage of Julian and Miss Alice takes place, Julian is filled with joy that he can serve his church and be married to Miss Alice at the same time. But then he finds that his bride has disappeared. "There I was . . . one moment married, flooded with white, and . . . then . . . the next, alone. Quite alone, in the . . . echoes." The Butler says sadly: "Like a little boy? When the closet door swings shut after him? Locking him in the dark? . . . And it's always remote, an attic closet, where one should not have been, where no one can hear, and is not likely to come . . . for a very long time."

(We are reminded that what happens in the castle also happens in the model, an *exact* repetition. Therefore, a wedding also took place in the model and a tiny Julian married a tiny Alice.)

Julian discovers that Miss Alice and the others have been packing and are about to leave without him. He is told that he is to be left to his marriage, his wife ("Alice"), and his special priesthood. He wants none of it; he wants *Miss* Alice. He is bewildered at the turn of events. He is horrified at what has taken place. He finds that he wants the concrete symbol, Miss Alice, not the abstraction "Alice." This is a terrible recognition: "All my life. In and out of . . . confinement, fought against the symbol."

Miss Alice tries to explain it to him and tells him to stay with "Alice," to accept the situation. He insists that he has married *Miss* Alice, but she replies: "No, Julian; you have married *her* . . . through me. . . . You are hers."

Julian refuses. He rushes to the model and shouts at it: "THERE IS NOTHING THERE!" Even when the Cardinal orders him, as a servant of the church, to accept his position as God's will, Julian refuses. Miss Alice tries to help him by saying: "Have done with forgery, Julian; accept what's real. I am the . . . illusion."

Julian persists in his stubbornness. When all persuasion fails, the Lawyer shoots him. He falls to the floor, mortally wounded. Miss Alice kneels to comfort him. She tells him he is like a little boy. He says that he is lonely. She asks, "Is being afraid always the same—no matter the circumstances, the age?" Julian answers: "It is the attic room, always; the closet. Hold close. . . . No one will come . . . for the longest time; if ever."

Miss Alice now consigns Julian to "Alice" and goes away. Julian is left to die alone. He relives the experience of the small child locked in an attic closet, with the family and servants out of hearing. The terror of abandonment is upon him. He cries out to God and immediately reminds himself that "THERE IS NO ONE!" He cries to God and to "Alice," seeming to confuse them in his agonized mind. While he is dying, we hear, faintly at first and growing louder, heartbeats and breathing. A "presence" seems to be entering the room. Julian continues in his monologue:

Alice? . . . God? SOMEONE? Come to Julian as he . . . ebbs. . . . Ah God! Is that the humor? THE ABTRACT? . . . REAL? THE REST? . . . FALSE? (*To himself, with terrible irony*) It is what I have wanted, have insisted on. Have nagged . . . for. (*Looking about the room, raging*) IS THIS MY PRIEST-HOOD, THEN? THIS WORLD? THEN COME AND SHOW THYSELF! BRIDE? GOD? . . . SHOW THYSELF! I DEMAND THEE! . . . SHOW THYSELF! FOR THEE I HAVE GAM-BLED . . . MY SOUL? I DEMAND THY PRESENCE. ALICE!

The sounds of breathing and the heartbeats become louder. In the model the light fades in the bedroom and begins to move across an upper story. Tiny Alice is coming down into the model room where tiny Julian lies. "Alice" is coming to Julian. He continues:

You . . . thou . . . art . . . coming to me? (*Frightened and angry*) ABSTRACTION? . . . ABSTRAC-TION! . . . (*Sad, defeated*) Art coming to me. . . . How long wilt thou forget me, O Lord? Forever? How long wilt thou hide thy face from me? . . . Consider and hear me, O Lord, my God. . . . CON-SIDER AND HEAR ME, O LORD, MY GOD. LIGHTEN MY EYES LEST I SLEEP THE SLEEP OF DEATH. . . . BUT I

HAVE TRUSTED IN THY MERCY, O LORD. HOW LONG WILT
THOU FORGET ME? . . . COME, BRIDE! COME, GOD!
COME! [The breathing and heartbeats are a great
deal louder.] Alice? (*Fear and trembling*) Alice?
ALICE? MY GOD, WHY HAST THOU FORSAKEN ME?

(*A great shadow, or darkening, fills the stage; it
is the shadow of a great presence filling the room.
The area on* JULIAN *and around him stays in some
light, but, for the rest, it is as if ink were moving
through paper toward a focal point. The sounds become enormous.* JULIAN *is aware of the presence in
the room, "sees" it, in the sense that his eyes, his
head move to all areas of the room, noticing his
engulfment. He almost-whispers loudly.*)

The bridegroom waits for thee, my Alice . . . is
thine. O Lord, my God, I have awaited thee, have
served thee in thy . . . ALICE? (*His arms are wide,
should resemble a crucifixion. With his hands on the
model, he will raise his body some, backed full up
against it*) ALICE? . . . GOD? (*The sounds are deaf-
ening. Julian smiles faintly*) I accept thee, Alice, for
thou are come to me. God, Alice . . . I accept thy
will. [The play closes with Albee's directions:]
(*Sounds continue.* JULIAN *dies, head bows, body relaxes some, arms stay wide in the crucifixion. Sounds
continue thusly: thrice after the death . . . thump*
thump *thump* thump *thump* thump. *Absolute silence
for two beats. The lights on* JULIAN *fade slowly to
black. Only then, when all is black, does the curtain
slowly fall.*)

There are, obviously, many ways of interpreting this
drama. Edward Albee reads widely, and he pours much
of his private symbolism into the play. We can find there
Freudian language and concepts, scenes and ideas taken

from Lewis Carroll's *Alice in Wonderland,* some of Carl Jung's mythological talk about archetypes, and intimations of the Gospels' story of Jesus' passion. It is quite impossible to weave all these sources into a simple meaningful whole. One must read or witness the drama and react to it from one's own experience and with one's own insight. It is a work of art that is to be grasped as a unity, a many-colored variation upon a basic theme.

Different explanations of this basic theme have been offered. Some interpreters feel that Julian typifies faith as an endless pilgrimage, that he continues his search for the true God until the end, that he does not give up his belief in the abstraction, does not accept a symbol—the concrete—as the best he can know. We can read the final speech as a triumphant cry of faithfulness and martyrdom: "I accept thee, Alice, for thou art come to me. God, Alice . . . I accept thy will." The Old Testament scholar, Samuel Terrien, takes this position. He calls Julian "a man of faith" who "calls for Alice and yet has not given up the real God."

A more profitable interpretation of the play is that Albee is not probing into the recesses of Christian faith, but is writing about modern man, who is bewildered by his position in a mysterious universe, who confuses illusion with reality, who does not know which of the many "worlds" or models is his own. This modern man employs abstract concepts, revealing a yearning for an abstract reality, for an experience of the ultimate.

In the play, Julian does not want the church's dogma about God, he wants what he calls the true God. He has fought all his life against symbols and dogmas in his desperate effort to serve only God himself. Thus Julian, a mortal creature, seeks the immortal, eternal ultimate.

But in the drama, he finds comfort and peace with Miss Alice. He loves her and believes that she loves him. They are married. He is satisfied. He wants to live with his wife and enjoy the relationship. He is no longer alone. At this point Albee slips in the dagger. Miss Alice is revealed to be a symbol for the abstract "Alice." Julian discovers that, although he has spent his life seeking the abstract truth, it is the material, living, warm, comforting symbol that has given him satisfaction. The irony is that his wish for the abstract is granted. Miss Alice is taken away from him and he is left alone, abandoned with his abstraction.

Albee seems to be saying that man may talk about abstractions, but that what he really wants, as man, is the concrete. A true human relationship is the best a man can expect on earth. If he insists upon the abstract, he can look forward only to disappointment.

Albee also seems to be saying that in an "expanding" universe modern man feels himself to be cosmically alone. He is like a small child who has wandered into an attic closet and accidentally closed and locked the door on himself. He cries and cries for help, but no one comes. The family is out; the servants are several floors below; no one hears. For the time that he is in the closet, the child feels alone in eternity. In that moment he is aware of the "anxiety of the infinite" that lies at the center of every human life. If one person will hear our cry and come to us in the closet and comfort us in our loneliness and fright, we are as fortunate as it is ever possible for man to be.

We cover our loneliness in the world with activity, sports, entertainment, drinking, drugs, fantasies, and the rest. Brother Julian refuses to delude himself with any of these means. But Albee insists that illusion is a necessity for life, since man cannot know an abstraction. Note again his words about *Tiny Alice:* "an examination of how much false illusion we need in order to get through life."

To Albee the "God we make in our own image" seems to be one of these false illusions necessary for existence to continue. But he presents us with Brother Julian, who has dedicated himself to living without the illusions and who insists on finding "the abstraction of God." When he lost his faith for six years and placed himself in a mental hospital, it was because he had temporarily accepted the world's view that illusions are necessary. When he regained his faith and his sanity, he continued his interrupted search.

In *Tiny Alice*, Albee is probing into the mystery of life. He knows the audience wants answers, a reaffirmation of its values. It wants to hear that the concrete and the abstract can be related in some meaningful way. But he considers himself an artist who must keep his integrity and mirror the confusion of modern man.

All of us who try to find legitimate goals in life are caught between the concrete and the abstract. Christians are not immune from this tension. For Christianity contains both Hebrew and Greek elements. Hebrew religion was concrete; it dealt with the "acts" of God. The Hebrew prophet witnessed to what God had done and was doing in history. If asked to describe the nature of God, the Hebrew told a story of God in action, e.g., freeing the Israelites from Egypt.

Greek philosophy, on the other hand, dealt with ideas, concepts, and mysteries. Plato talked about "ideals," eternal in the heavens, that were reflected in concrete phenomena. There is an ideal table that is the essence of "tableness"; there are many concrete tables in the world. The Greek philosopher described God in terms of abstract qualities—omnipotence, omnipresence, transcendence, omniscience.

So we find ourselves constantly dealing with the problem of how to know God. Is he recognized in our history, in our experience, or is he known "out there" as an abstraction?

7
THE
HOSTILE ENVIRONMENT

BENEATH THE SURFACE OF "POLITE SOCIETY" IS THE BATTLE-field. Men and women know the deadly conflict that takes place in the business organization, the professions, and the government. For the ambitious individual, it is dangerous to enter where the competition is strong. There are many wounded emotionally and physically in the battle; there are some who are killed.

Rod Serling wrote an excellent television drama some years ago entitled *Patterns*. He uncovered the struggle for power within a large business corporation in New York City. The president wished to remove from office the first vice-president, whom he thought to be un-creative and behind the times. Not wishing to ask for the man's resignation because of his long service in the company and his popularity among his colleagues, the president undertook to keep this man under a severe pressure of criticism and, at times, ridicule. But the man was a fighter and refused to give in and resign. He developed an ulcer, and his general health declined until he was a shadow of his former self. Then, after a particularly stormy session in a meeting with the president, he had a heart attack and died. This man had experienced life on "the killing ground."

Often the killing ground is not concealed from public view. We read in the newspapers of riots in our cities, of bombing and burnings, of murders. We hear of gang fights and battles between the police and hoodlums. All the repressed hostilities of underprivileged people burst out during the long, hot summer, and violence is visible. Frightened citizens buy guns and prepare to defend themselves from attack.

We hear of mass murders: Five women were slain in New Jersey in less than a year. A disturbed student killed fifteen persons and wounded thirty-two more as he shot down at them from the tower of a Texas university. Two young men wiped out a family on a farm in Kansas. Eight student nurses were killed by a man in Chicago.

The twentieth century is an age of violence. Two great world wars and many smaller wars have destroyed millions of lives. Today we live under the threat of atomic destruction and have so lived for so many years that we have come to take it for granted.

As civilized, even Christian, people, we want to believe that human beings are gentle and cooperative at heart. We consider violence abnormal and against the true nature of man. We feel that peace is the usual condition of international life and that war is a sickness, an interruption of peace. But the evidence of our times

makes clear that conflict and hostility are constantly
present in human life. Sigmund Freud's studies of the
human unconscious revealed the aggressions and hostilities that lurk within all of us, straining to be released,
and held in check by the moral and social restraints of
civilization. Man's instincts and his conscience are in
constant tension.

Konrad Lorenz, a perceptive student of animal and
human behavior, has written a book entitled *On Aggression,* in which he spells out the basic difference between
animal and human aggression. Animals fight one another
for a mate, food, an area of dominion; they do not fight
to kill. When one animal is defeated in a battle, he offers
his throat to the other for the *coup de grâce.* The victor
turns away, and the defeated leaves the field of battle
and disappears. Animals kill one another for food, but
never to prove superiority in fighting. On the other hand,
Lorenz points out, humans do fight to kill. Aggression,
which is partial among animals, is total among men.
Humans do not kill other men for food; they kill to
clinch their victory.

William Hanley/*Slow Dance on the Killing Ground*

William Hanley, who was born in 1931 and lived
through his most impressionable years during the Second
World War, has been deeply moved by the experience
of violence in our era. He has written a perceptive
drama, *Slow Dance on the Killing Ground,* to probe into
some of the implications of this widespread aggression.

The play takes place on one evening, June 1, 1962, in

a small candy store situated in a warehouse and factory district in Brooklyn, New York. Although the area teems with workers during the day, at night it is silent and dark, the streetlamps unlighted.

The candy store is managed by a man named Glas. He is white, about sixty-five years old, walks with a limp, and is usually silent, although he absorbs all that happens around him.

The action begins when Randall, a young Negro, rushes in from the dark street. He is about eighteen, slim and handsome. He is dressed in the Edwardian style popular among young people of the day. It is obvious that Randall has escaped from something threatening "out there." He is nervous and talks compulsively—mostly about himself. Randall claims to have an I.Q. of 187 and to have been in trouble in various schools because he was too bright for the teachers. He is bitter about the fact that his color has made it impossible for him to use his intelligence successfully. He has a lively imagination and is having trouble with his identity. Over the years, he discloses, he has changed his name. For a time he called himself Winston. Then he selected Franz (for Franz Kafka). At present he is considering calling himself Maximilian, after the French emperor of Mexico.

Randall talks with Glas about the nature of life "out there" in the dark streets of Brooklyn. They agree that it is dangerous. Randall makes a long speech that reveals the theme of the play:

It is grotesque out there, ain't it now? It is . . . *bizarre!* You know what that is out there, daddy? You know? That is the *killing* ground out there.

. . . I mean that's no man's land out there, daddy! That somebody *else's* turf, a regular *mine field,* you gotta step *care*fully, they *kill* you out there. . . . Butcher shop. It a regular butcher shop out there. You know what happened out there just last year alone? . . . Four hundred and eighty-three homicides! . . . "Three hundred and ninety-seven of the victims were over twenty-one; thirty-four were under seven. One hundred and thirteen of the victims were women; ninety-eight women were arrested for homicide. . . . Fifteen husbands were slain by their wives. Eighteen wives were slain by their husbands . . . ten sons were slain by their mothers . . . two sons were slain by their fathers . . . six daughters were slain by their mothers . . . four daughters were slain by their fathers . . . one father was killed by his daughter . . . two mothers were killed by their sons . . . two sisters killed their brothers . . . one despondent mother drowned her three children in the East River . . . another despondent mother drowned her three children in a bathtub . . . one child was killed for bedwetting . . . " Oh, man, man . . .[36]

It is obvious that Randall has memorized the crime statistics for the last year in the city. Glas and he talk about the recent execution of the Nazi Eichmann for his crimes against the Jews during World War II. Glas shrugs off the enormity of it all. He does not wish to become involved. "I stay right here and I watch the world go by and I don't get in its way."

[36] This quotation and those which follow are from *Slow Dance on the Killing Ground,* by William Hanley (Random House, Inc.). Copyright © 1964 by William Hanley. Reprinted by permission of Random House, Inc.

Randall insists that one cannot ignore the world. Sooner or later the world is going to come in the door of the candy store with a gun in its hand. In that case, says Glas, he, too, has a gun. He shows Randall the revolver he keeps under the counter. (It is not loaded.) After he has seen the gun, Randall smiles: "Well now, well now. I thought you wasn't a member of the club, you been sayin'. You a member in good standin', dues all paid up."

Glas unthaws a bit and tells something of his own background. He says he was a Communist in Germany and spent some time in a concentration camp, where the Nazis broke his leg in four places, "Starting at the ankle and working their way up." He was angered in his soul by the violence of the Nazi regime and claims to Randall that the Nazis are still present. In fact, he claims that Nazis put the juke box in his candy store:

That monstrosity, that noise box. What do you think it's doing here? One day two men come in and look around and ask me how would I like a juke box, give the place a little class? I say no, thanks just the same, I don't need no juke boxes today. They say, sure I do, they can tell just by looking at me that I need a juke box. I say no, still very polite. They say yes, only not so nice this time. I say no again, they say yes, I say definitely no. So the next night a brick through the window, glass flying all over the place, a cut on my head. So I have a juke box. And those men, they wear white ties with their black shirts, but around the eyes—just like the Nazis.

Glas knows what violence is. He wants nothing to do with it. He hopes to escape notice by being quiet and not stirring up trouble. Randall feels that they both understand the nature of "the killing ground." He tells Glas something of his background. He has no home; he wanders around the city sleeping where he can. His mother was a prostitute and he was born with a congenital condition that he calls "a hole in my heart." He explains it: "Conceived of lust and the natural hungers of the flesh, but without love. It was that absence of love that left the hole in Randall's heart, no mistake."

While they are talking, a girl bursts into the store. She is white, about nineteen, plain-looking, with eyeglasses and orange hair. She is dressed in a pullover, blue denim skirt, and sandals. Her name is Rosie. She says she wants to know the location of the Brooklyn Bridge. After some questioning, she says she wants to find the bridge and jump. She has been searching for a doctor whose address she has been given, but she has not been able to find the number in the dark streets. With some hesitation, she admits that she is pregnant and that the doctor is an abortionist.

Randall is curious about her background and persuades her to tell them her story. She says that her father was killed in the Second World War and that her mother married again. She does not get along with her stepfather, who is ambitious and hardworking. The family has moved up socially until they live in a pleasant apartment in the Riverdale section of the Bronx, an exclusive area. In rebellion, Rosie has had a brief and messy affair with a college boy.

Randall and Rosie, as young people in a frightening world, try to communicate with each other, but their natural suspicions are so great that they cannot relate to each other with any success. Each remains a stranger and alone.

Then Randall turns to Glas and asks him to tell the real story of his life. He accuses Glas of pretending to be an observer of life while really struggling to survive. His passivity, charges Randall, is his strategy for survival. Glas sidesteps by reminding Randall that "they kill you out there." To which Randall replies: "We're all going to fall on the killing ground one day or another, Mister Glas. At least, I'll die in action. And it's you who has the gun, remember? You're in no position to look with contempt upon those of us who choose to defend ourselves: it's *you* who has the gun."

Rosie breaks in to say she would like to save life, not destroy. She would save Randall's life if he were in danger. He turns to her: "All right, I'm dying. Save me." She tries to understand his words. He adds, "I'm what the psychologists call a 'unreachable youth.' You tryin' to reach me?"

She struggles against the pessimism of the two men. Glas insists that "nobody saves nobody." Rosie feels this is inhuman. Glas turns on her: "You want to save somebody, Rosie? Save *that* life [the unborn child within her], then! Save what you *can* save." She turns a deaf ear to his plea. It is clear that she is interested in the idea of "saving" others in general, but not in the particular act of saving a life that is her responsibility.

Glas then recounts the real story of his life and how he

discovered, when it was too late, that he could not save
the people he loved. In Germany he had married a
Jewish woman and they had brought a son into the
world. When the Nazis came to power, Glas, his wife,
and son were all considered Jewish. In 1938 he saw the
handwriting on the wall and decided to leave his family
and fight the Nazis as a Communist. "I abandoned them,
my wife and my child, in the middle of the night, without a word. I went to another city, I took another name.
All for the Party, for the glorious cause."

He worked as a railroad engineer and soon found himself carrying Jews to the concentration camp at Maut-
hausen. Then came the pact between Hitler and Stalin.
Glas was horrified. He felt he had left his family and
worked for the Party for nothing—"My god kissed Satan
and called him friend." He hurried back to his home,
only to find the house ransacked and his family gone. He
was filled with remorse and a longing to be punished for
his crime against those he loved. To Rosie, Glas says:
"Save what you *can* save, Rosie. I know."

Glas then admits that he was never in a concentration
camp himself. His leg was broken, not by the Nazis but
in a railroad accident. He tells the others that he envies
Eichmann, the murderer of thousands, because he has
been caught and brought to judgment. His days of waiting are over. But, Glas asks, "Who will judge *me?* Who
will condemn *me,* and by what law?" He walks out of
the store in despair.

Randall sees Glas as a man whose desperate need is
to be judged. Randall arranges the room as a court. He is

to be the judge and Rosie the jury. When the older man returns, Randall accuses him of abandoning his family and of knowingly transporting Jews to their death. Glas pleads guilty on both counts. Randall then digs deeper into the case and accuses Glas of continuing to live after he realized what he had done. He did not seek out punishment, but withdrew from the field of battle. Again Glas admits his guilt.

Acting as the judge, Randall condemns Glas to death. He takes Glas's revolver, puts it to the older man's temple, and pulls the trigger. But the revolver, of course, is unloaded.

Randall has done what he can for Glas. He would like to do something for Rosie. He begs her to allow her child to live. She refuses and asks both of them to understand how she feels.

Randall expresses *his* feelings: "There is a *passion* loose in the world! A passion for the sounds of violence, for the sight of pain! A passion for death and disaster! We're up to the eyeballs in blood, little chick: you gotta swim in it or drown in it. . . . It's a butcher shop, little Rosie! *Where's your cleaver!*"

Glas feels that there is something behind Randall's violent feelings. He asks the youth to explain what has happened to him. Randall unfolds a bloody and violent account of how, that same evening, he has murdered his prostitute mother with a knife and an ice pick. She had neglected and abandoned him. She cared only for herself. His hatred for her created the murderous violence within him.

Rosie is shaken by his story and terrified for him. She hopes he can escape the police. Randall is somewhat amused: "I have broken the laws of God and Man, you're supposed to want to see me apprehended and brought before the bar of justice and be delivered up to mine executioners."

Rosie does not care what she is supposed to want. She knows Randall and she wants him to live. He says that he left fingerprints everywhere in the room where the murder took place and that others in the house recognized him. She wants to know what they can *do*. Randall shakes his head and asks Glas to explain it to her. Quietly Glas speaks:

> Don't you see, Rosie . . . Randall must die now, violently, because of what he is and because of what he has done. And I will *live*, without violence, because of what I am and what I have done. And you, Rosie . . . you will go to your doctor, up that dark street, and afterward . . . you will write books, maybe . . . about how people should save each other . . . We choose, Rosie. We choose the dark streets up which we walk. . . . And if we are guilty of the denial of life . . . who is there to save us from that . . . but ourselves?

Randall decides it is time for him to go out. If he is caught, he will fight and be killed. He looks out the door: "Man! Man! I sure don't like it out there."

LeRoi Jones / *The Toilet* and *Dutchman*

Another man who "does not like it out there" is the black playwright LeRoi Jones. As one who has been involved in the hysterical violence of urban race riots, he has experienced the senselessness of sheer hostility let loose among a mass of frustrated people. It may be that because we live between cultures human beings are bewildered and turn to violence as a way of expressing their confusion and resentment at not having life clearly structured for them.

A professor of government at Columbia University, Dr. Zbigniew Brzezinski, has dealt with the rise of violence in our culture in his book, *Between Two Ages*. As is obvious to all of us, living in the period between cultures brings almost intolerable pressures, pain, and a growing demand for direction. Out of the dislocation of our era comes the desire to "drop out" of society and return to a more simple age when things made sense and the pattern of life was easy to comprehend. But in history there is no turning back. To opt out means to become obsolete and, thus, ignored by the process of cultural change and development. As Dr. Brzenzinski explains, we have come to the end of the age of industrialism and are entering what he calls the "technetronic era." He uses this term because he feels that the principal impulses of change today are technology and electronics. It is one thing to be a professor of government and to make profound observations on the passing scene; it is quite another thing to be involved in social changes without having the larger view and yet having to endure the suffering and frustration of lostness.

In our nation, we have become an urban people. The city began as our home and a place of opportunity for the exercise of talent, but it has become an asphalt jungle. As we look at the great city today, we see that it is practically ungovernable—it is a horde of people trying to exist, of incoherence, congestion, and violence. Under the circumstances, it is no coincidence that the crime rate in the United States has risen 148 percent in the last decade. It is reported that five million known crimes were committed in 1969, and only 50 percent of all crimes were reported to the police. In 1969, violence appeared on three major fronts: there were 14,950 murders, 9,414 individuals were killed in Indochina, and 56,400 were killed in traffic accidents. These figures bring home to us the magnitude of the violence in our supposedly civilized society.

Into this turbulent situation have come the people from minority groups—the blacks from the agricultural south and the Spanish-Americans from Puerto Rico and other Spanish-speaking areas. They moved into our large cities to escape from rural poverty and to find an economic future for themselves and their children. Lacking money and social mobility, they have found themselves crowded into the violent slums of our urban areas. The "propaganda" of a democratic society has urged them to better themselves by adjusting to the ways of the majority and accepting the customs and values of the dominant group. In reality, they have found little welcome in the supposedly "open society" and have been blocked by the same institutions that urge them to advance.

LeRoi Jones knows what it is like to exist in the urban jungle. He is aware of the fact that although we like to think of ourselves as a gracious, peace-loving people, we are actually violence prone and demonstrate atavism toward force in all our mass media and in the way we actually behave toward one another daily. His short play *The Toilet* [37] is a demonstration of how young boys are initiated into this culture of violence.

The scene is the boys' rest room in a deteriorating slum school. The room has walls of gray rough cement, the floor is wet, the place smells. It is to this room that the male students repair when they have business to transact on their own without interference from teachers or the school administration. As the play begins, we discover that a gang of boys is gathering in the toilet to witness a fight between their leader, Foots, and an outsider, Karolis, who has insulted Foots by sending him a letter saying that he thinks the gang leader is "beautiful."

Several boys have been sent to capture Karolis and bring him down to the rest room. While they are waiting for him, the others insult one another and engage in a constant punching. They seem to have to prove their manhood by hitting and cursing. Finally, when Karolis has been captured and brought in, it is obvious that he

[37] In the Evergreen Playscript, *The Baptism & The Toilet,* by LeRoi Jones (Grove Press, Inc., 1967).

has already been beaten by his captors and is in no condition for a fight with Foots. However, egged on by the
others, Karolis insists upon fighting.

Foots tries to avoid the battle because of Karolis'
beaten condition, but Karolis says he wants to fight; he
wants to kill Foots, whom he calls by his real name, Ray.
Karolis reminds Ray that he had sent him the letter saying he was beautiful and that he loved him. This starts
the fight in earnest. Karolis leaps upon Foots and gets a
sudden stranglehold which the other cannot break. Suddenly, the others rush upon them, drag Karolis off his
victim, throw him to the floor, and surge around him,
punching him in the face. After a few moments, Foots
comes back into the room, stares at Karolis' body, looks
quickly over his shoulder, then runs and kneels before
the body, weeping and cradling the head in his arms as
the play ends.

This violent, raging drama makes it clear that to be
manly and accepted in the urban adolescent society a
boy must be tough, ready to hit or to curse, willing to
use violence to demonstrate his masculinity. If there is
sensitivity and a feeling of tenderness for another human
being, it must never be allowed to show. Alone with
Karolis, Foots can be kind and warm, but never when
others are about. In the gang, punching is the way they
relate to one another. The play is a forceful illustration
of Reinhold Niebuhr's thesis of "moral man in immoral
society."

This urban adolescent model of masculinity as always
harsh and tough distorts the true human concept of man-
liness, in which strength is blended with responsibility

for others and with empathy. The true strong man does not have to "prove" his manhood over and over. But this is something these boys know nothing about. To express tenderness is an insult to the other person, and a fight must result.

We are horrified to read in the newspapers that a group of boys have beaten an old man to death as he sat on a secluded park bench. Would any one of them commit this crime alone? What are they trying to prove? Where does this brutality come from?

The inner city seems to resemble a jungle that fosters a return to bestiality on the part of young men. It brings out the bloodlust in these groups of boys. We know that this same distorted idea of manhood obtains also in exclusive private schools and military academies. It seems to be a fact of our society itself. This forces us to ask ourselves: Does our culture present to the young a distorted image of manhood as tough, violent, and unfeeling? Is this the message of our mass media? Does the popular television program and the successful motion picture glorify the tough male who fights and brawls his way to his goal?

LeRoi Jones is saying to us in this short play that our violent society is producing distorted adolescents who are afraid of tenderness. The youthful code of violence is a reflection of a culture that seems to honor toughness. It is in such a world as this that the church seeks to create a Christian, a truly human, community. Jones is an angry prophet in our day who pictures vividly for us the dehumanizing of youth by an age of violence.

The problem for the black man in this era between

two ages is more aggravating than for the rest of us. He not only experiences all the fears and frustrations of a rapidly changing time, but he also has to face the hidden, but well-organized, opposition of the majority group in power. LeRoi Jones, in his drama *Dutchman*,[38] succeeds in revealing the paradoxes of our society as it both encourages and blocks black men and women.

Dutchman, a violent, fast-moving, incisive short drama won the Obie Award as the best American play of the 1963–1964 season. In it we find LeRoi Jones describing graphically and passionately the tragic experience of the black man in our white American society.

The scene is part of the inside of a New York subway car. There are but two main characters: Clay, a well-dressed, handsome young black man, and Lula, a young and attractive red-haired white woman. As the play begins, Lula enters the car and sits down next to Clay. She begins a conversation. She is provocative; he is cautious. Suddenly, she asks him what he is prepared for. Clay, taken by surprise at this probing, holds her off by answering, in a bantering way, that he is prepared for anything and challenges her for a suggestion. She ignores his question and begins to make fun of him for his conservative clothing and careful appearance. She guesses that he lives in New Jersey with his parents, reads Chinese poetry and drinks lukewarm, sugarless tea. He laughs and agrees she may have some of the picture correct, Lula teases him and eggs him on with a some-

[38] *Dutchman* is found in *New Theatre in America,* edited by Edward Parone (Dell Publishing Co., Inc., 1965).

what cruel relentlessness. She increases the tension sharply by asking him if he would like to get involved with her.

Clay continues to play it lightly and says it would be all right with him. She guesses that he is on his way to a party and asks to go along. He agrees to take her, whereupon she turns on him and tells him sharply not to get smart with her. She heightens the attack with harsh criticism of his appearance. She accuses him of wearing clothes that come from the very tradition that is oppressing him. She asks him what right he thinks he has to wear a business suit and a striped tie when his grandfather was a slave who obviously did not go to Harvard. Clay refuses to become angry; he keeps his cool. Lula then digs beneath the surface of his appearance and demeanor to announce loudly that he is a murderer and that he knows it.

There is a brief interruption while other passengers appear in the subway car. Then the conversation continues between the two. They plan how they will go to the party together and then move on to Lula's room. In this exchange, she excites Clay and then angers him. She leads him on and then attacks him. He is suddenly aware of the other passengers; she asks him if they frighten him because he knows he is really "an escaped nigger." She jumps up in the aisle and begins to dance. She loudly invites him to join her. Clay tries to quiet her and to persuade her to sit down. She refuses and cries that he has to learn to break out. She accuses him of just sitting and allowing society to kill him. She urges him to get up and assert himself as a man. Finally angry, Clay forces her into a seat and slaps her across the mouth.

Then Clay begins to let out his true feelings. He tells her that he could murder her at that very moment. He glares at the other passengers who are staring at him over their newspapers and says that their weak white faces make him want to murder them too. He tells Lula to shut up. He knows he is a fake white man in a middle-class disguise. He declares that he sits there and holds himself in so that he will not cut all their throats. He states flatly that murder would make them all sane. Lula has been trying to provoke just this kind of revealing outburst, so she is somewhat satisfied.

Clay warms to his topic and suggests that Lula give her father a message from him: Don't preach rational-ism and try to be logical when talking with blacks. Clay suggests that the whites leave them alone and let the blacks sing their curses in code. He points out that if the whites succeed in convincing the blacks that Western culture is the best and that they ought to become com-pletely part of it, then the blacks may well become "stand-up Western men, with eyes for clean, hard, use-ful lives, sober, pious, and sane." Then, announces Clay, they will murder the whites and have sound rational explanations. The most dangerous thing for whites to do, therefore, is to convert the blacks to their own seemingly intellectual, but actually violent, way of life.

At this point, Lula changes her approach. She tells Clay abruptly that she has heard enough. He decides to get off at the next stop and bends over to pick up his belongings, which have slipped to the floor. Lula pulls a knife out of her bag and suddenly stabs him twice in the chest. He slumps, dead, across her knees. She commands the passengers to get him off her and to throw his body off the train between the cars. She orders them all to get off at the next stop. Her commands are obeyed. She is left alone in the subway car.

Very soon a young black man of about twenty enters the car and sits a few seats away from Lula. She moves over near him and stares at him until he looks at her. Satisfied that he is showing interest, Lula smiles to herself as the curtain falls.

In this brief drama, we watch Clay pass through the various stages of Negro history in America. He has struggled out of a poverty culture and tried with all his might and mind to adapt to the white society. He dresses, talks, studies, behaves, like a white man. He finds he is tolerated and baited. The white society has told him that if he would adapt, he would be accepted. But Clay finds this to be a lie. When he is goaded into honestly expressing his feelings, he is killed by the same white person who had seemed to welcome him.

LeRoi Jones seems to be saying that white society lures the black man into its rationalizations in order to betray him. The black man is praised for his good sense, his songs, his humor, and his willingness to please—and then made to feel a fool for his efforts. He is taunted until his honest anger bursts out. This, of course, justifies using violence against him. We must have "order in the streets." Lula leads Clay on until he is so frustrated,

frightened, and furious that he betrays his true feelings
. . . which produces her response: "I've heard enough."
And then the knife.

Jones also helps us to understand that the sex talk
and imagery have little to do with love and tenderness.
Sex, too, is a form of violence. Lula uses sex as a weapon,
an instrument of torture. She is excited by the myth of
black masculinity and tries to force Clay to declare his
physical passion in a game of sexual fantasy. But when
he ventures to play her game, she coldly rebuffs him
with, "Don't get smart with me, Buster."

By various means, white society provokes black men
to express their anger in violence in order to justify
using violence against them. This has been LeRoi Jones's
experience in our society. This process is most obvious
in our urban riots of late. Jones faced the process himself in Newark, his hometown.

Like Lula and Clay, all of us in our culture know how
to provoke one another to murder. The very violence we
decry is what we create.

These plays present a picture of life that is not pretty.
But one must know the reality of his times. Are we not all
at the mercy of the violence of our generation? Are we
not part of that violence in our not caring? How does a
person live with his sense of guilt? Can any one of us
save another or even forgive him?

Polite, kindly individuals have an aversion to being
told that beneath the surface of civilized life is "the
killing ground." This sounds brutal, inhuman, pessimistic,
perverse. They want to turn away and pretend that they
have not seen it.

This same blindness is to be found among Christians who exalt the Sermon on the Mount, the healing of the sick, the compassion of Jesus—and avoid the hostility to him that culminated in mocking, whipping, and crucifixion.

The churches are crowded on Palm Sunday as the triumphal entry into Jerusalem is celebrated. The crowds appear again on Easter when the glorious resurrection of Christ is celebrated. But the crowds are strangely absent on Good Friday when the bitter event of the crucifixion is remembered.

Jesus of Nazareth, who spent his short life moving about among men doing good, was killed—murdered by "good" men who felt that he was a menace to their way of life. The crucifixion is the central evidence of man's inhumanity to man. The man of peace met violence from the men of the world. We cannot understand the Christian gospel, with its fundamental emphasis on the resurrection, if we do not take the crucifixion seriously—and personally.

Søren Kierkegaard, the Danish theologian of a century ago, said that the true Christian is one who is *contemporary* with Jesus, not one who celebrates the "Christ of glory."

To be contemporary with Jesus means to be a follower of the Jesus of Nazareth who was an outcast, who was hunted and despised, who was finally put to death upon a cross between two common criminals. To be his contemporary means to be willing to be an outcast with him, to be willing to chance a personal crucifixion.

But to celebrate the Christ of glory is to be one who

follows the crowd to church as a conventional thing to do, who feels that Christianity is important for successful living in society. As Kierkegaard insisted: Where everyone is a Christian, no one is a Christian.

8
EXISTENCE
BETWEEN CULTURES

TODAY WE LIVE IN THAT TORMENTING TIME, THE FORMLESS era between cultures. As we look back, we can see the rise and fall of the Greco-Roman Age, the Medieval Age, and what we have called the Modern Age. Our culture, which developed out of the Enlightenment, the Renaissance, the Reformation, and the Scientific-Technological explosion, came to its high point at the opening of the twentieth century and has been in decline for some decades. The social structures that supported this "modern culture" have crumbled and new structures have not yet made their appearance. The institutions that gave form to our society—families, schools, churches, governments—are in trouble if not actually broken down. The onetime "eternal verities" are no longer recognized as lasting or even true.

It is becoming plain to us that modern man is obsolete. The "new" man is not yet clear to us. History has speeded up like a motion picture projector suddenly accelerating so that the characters on the screen rush about in triple tempo. Constant change, startling new developments and the need for rapid readjustment have produced in many of us the reaction that Alvin Toffler calls "Future Shock." This is a painful awareness of stress and disorientation as we find ourselves subjected to too much change in too short a time.

There are some persons today who refuse to believe that men have landed on the moon. They consider the entire adventure to be a television trick. They cannot endure the shock of believing that space travel is a reality. All of us have our methods of retreating from the stress of constant change.

Richard Rovere has written that our modern world "is so very different that fathers cannot convince grown sons—young men born into that other world—that the place (1948) ever existed or that its terrors were real." He goes on to say: "We have become a different people, some of us who recall 1948 being frighteningly estranged from our former selves. Our society has a different structure, different values, different aims."

In the light of these facts, what does it "feel like" to be alive in this explosively changing age? When asked this question, individuals have responded with two seemingly opposite reactions: exhilaration and near panic. It is an exciting time to be alive; it is a frightening time. There is an undefined quality about our existence. There is a rush of new idealism and a drain of dark cynicism. Old values have been rejected; the search is on for new values. Absolute moral standards are being shaken by the relative standards of situation ethics. Individual worth seems lost, yet there is a new sense of togetherness related to the rise of a new kind of tribalism. Communication between people is difficult if not impossible. It is hard to find a firm place upon which to stand. Change is so constant and far-reaching that frustration and confusion are daily companions. It is a great time to be alive; it is a terrible time to be alive.

TOM STOPPARD/*Rosencrantz & Guildenstern Are Dead*

Once we understand what it *feels like* to exist in the second half of the twentieth century, we can comprehend what the playwright is trying to say to us in a drama which often seems to us to be absurd. It is his hope that we shall be able to comprehend emotionally the meaning of being alive. This is the purpose of Tom Stoppard in his fascinating play *Rosencrantz & Guildenstern Are Dead*. A young British actor and dramatist, Stoppard has brought to vivid life a number of themes found in our era between cultures.

Those who are acquainted with Shakespeare's *Hamlet* will remember that Rosencrantz and Guildenstern are two minor characters in that great drama. They had been fellow students with Hamlet in the University of Wittenberg. When Hamlet returned to Denmark after his father's sudden death, he found his mother, the queen, already married to her brother-in-law. Hamlet suspected foul play. In the eyes of the king and queen, he was acting strangely. He was melancholy and distraught. The royal couple sent for Rosencrantz and Guildenstern to come to the castle in Elsinore in order to find out the trouble with Hamlet and to cheer him up, if possible. In the original drama, the two young men appear and try to make contact with Hamlet. He is cordial to them, but does not confide in them because he believes, quite rightly, that what he says to them will be repeated to the king and queen. When it is obvious that Hamlet is suspicious of his foster father, the king arranges to have the two friends accompany Hamlet to England where the prince is to be executed. A sealed letter to the English sovereign contains the death order. During the voyage, Hamlet rewrites the letter which he leaves with the two men and escapes. The two make their way to England without Hamlet and, upon arrival, are killed.

Stoppard retells the story of Hamlet with the two young men as the central characters. All of the scenes in which the two appear in the original Shakespearean tragedy are included but most of the time is given to what takes place "offstage" in the lives of these two friends. The play makes sense when one realizes that Stoppard is using this convention to make us aware of what it is like to live in our own time. By removing us from our century and taking us back to Shakespeare's Elsinore in the seventeenth century, he gives us the platform upon which to stand as we observe the passing scene. We feel safe in history and can listen and look without severe anxiety. But although these characters are dressed in Elizabethan costumes, they are modern young men afflicted with all the problems we face to-day.

Rosencrantz and Guildenstern are minor characters in

Hamlet but they become the main personages here. To-day is the age of the common man. Royalty has faded from the scene. Great men do not dominate events. The George Pattons give way to the Omar Bradleys. The organization is central and men work as parts of the whole. The "heroes" of our time are the common participants. It would be difficult for us to feel at home with Prince Hamlet of the royal house of Denmark; it is easy for us to identify with the visiting students, Rosencrantz and Guildenstern. As we consider the text of the drama, we find familiar themes appearing.

At the opening of the play, the two men are on the road going to Elsinore. To pass the time, they are tossing coins. If a coin comes down heads, it goes to one of them; if it lands tails, it goes to the other. But a curious thing has taken place—ninety-two coins have been spun consecutively and all have come down heads. Obviously the law of probability is not working. We are immediately aware of a feeling of uneasiness. This is close to home. In our modern world, the onetime accepted laws of classical physics no longer obtain in the emerging era of atomic or nuclear physics. All standards and values are questioned. As the coins spin, we feel that the times are out of joint.

Rosencrantz and Guildenstern talk over the events of the day. Early in the morning they were awakened by a stranger who rode his horse under their window and, standing on his saddle, banged on the shutters and shouted their names. From him they learned that they had been sent for—by Denmark's king and queen. Says Rosencrantz: "It was urgent—a matter of extreme ur-

gency, a royal summons, his very words: official business
and no questions asked—lights in the stable-yard, saddle
up and off headlong and hotfoot across the land, our
guides outstripped in breakneck pursuit of our duty!
Fearful lest we come too late!" [39]

Too late for what? is the question. Neither knows.
They are not sure of the direction. They have been
summoned, for what? In confusion, Guildenstern tries
to sort out what has happened to them: "Practically
starting from scratch. . . . An awakening, a man standing on his saddle to bang on the shutters, our names
shouted in a certain dawn, a message, a summons. . . .
A new record for heads and tails. We have not been
. . . picked out . . . simply to be abandoned . . . set
loose to find our own way. . . . We are entitled to
some direction . . . I would have thought."

A constant thought of our own, is it not? Each of us
was called into existence and his name was "called" when
it was written upon the birth certificate and spoken in
the moment of baptism. Each of us has been summoned
into the world, but for what purpose? Many young persons today feel they have been abandoned, set loose to
find their own way. They, too, resent the fact that they
have not been given some definite direction. The experience of being summoned and setting out upon a
journey without a map is thoroughly modern.

On the road, the two friends come upon a troupe of
actors also on their way to Elsinore where they hope to

[39] This quotation and those which follow are from *Rosencrantz
& Guildenstern Are Dead,* by Tom Stoppard (Grove Press, Inc.).
Copyright © 1967 by Tom Stoppard. Used by permission of Grove
Press, Inc.

perform for the court. The leader of the actors talks with the two travelers about his profession and is asked about what he actually does. The player responds: "We keep to our usual stuff, more or less, only inside out. We do onstage the things that are supposed to happen off. Which is a kind of integrity, if you look on every exit being an entrance somewhere else."

This is the way in which Stoppard has conceived of his play. In Shakespeare's *Hamlet* when Rosencrantz and Guildenstern exit, they cease to exist for the playwright and for the audience. Stoppard, in this drama, creates that offstage existence. The two Wittenberg students have lives of their own and are important in terms of themselves. Attention must be paid to them if we are to take seriously the human individual. In our own experience, it is difficult for us to be completely aware of the lives others live beyond our sight and knowledge. When they are "offstage" in the sense that they are not an active part in our own lives, we tend to feel that they do not really exist until their next entrance into our experience. For a young child, it is a shock to discover that his mother has a life in any way separated from him. An older man, looking back, said that it came to him as a startling awakening when as a child of three he looked out of his nursery window and saw his mother playing croquet on the lawn. He felt somehow betrayed that she should have a life in which he was not the center. It is part of the maturing process in our relationships with others to be able "to look on every exit being an entrance somewhere else."

Rosencrantz and Guildenstern arrive at Elsinore and

are entertained by the king and queen, who tell them of Hamlet's seeming illness and ask them to try to find out what is wrong so they can help the prince. When they are again alone, the two young men talk over the situation. They feel they appeared ridiculous before the royal pair; they simply scraped and bowed and failed to express any reactions of their own. One cries out: "Consistency is all I ask!" and the other answers: "Give us this day our daily mask." They have nothing but appearances to go on. They want to leave but they do not know where to go. They have lost their sense of direction. Guildenstern points out: "The only beginning is birth and the only end is death—if you can't count on that, what can you count on?"

They remember that in school the teachers asked questions to which there were always answers. One grows up believing that there *are* correct answers. But then, in adult life, one runs up against the fact that there are many questions without answers. One has to make decisions and take his chances. The two friends try to find a form of security in the fact that they have been given instructions by the king and queen.

GUILDENSTERN: We've been caught up. Your smallest action sets off another somewhere else, and is set off by it. Keep an eye open, an ear cocked. Tread warily, follow instructions. We'll be all right.

ROSENCRANTZ: For how long?

GUILDENSTERN: Till events have played themselves out. There's a logic at work—it's all done for you, don't worry. Enjoy it. Relax. To be taken in hand and led, like being a child again, even without the

innocence, a child—it's like being given a prize,
an extra slice of childhood when you least expect it.

In all of us there is this, at times, this intense desire
to return to the certitude of childhood when there were
answers, when actions were clearly right or wrong,
where parents and teachers made plans for one. But to
grow up and to take responsibility for one's own life,
especially in an era between cultures, brings one face to
face with uncertainty and a dearth of answers.

The two men discuss how they will deal with Hamlet
when they finally meet him. They role-play the situation,
but are most unhappy with the results. They realize
they simply do not know how to go about the business
of finding out what is wrong in order to explain it to
the king and queen that Hamlet may be healed. This,
too, is a common human predicament. How do we come
to understand one another? There are those in emotional trouble who need our help. We struggle with an
attempt to comprehend what is wrong and to make
tentative suggestions for improvement, all the time
feeling that we are fumbling in the dark. It is a dis-
turbing matter to be asked to interfere in the life of
another.

The company of actors have arrived at Elsinore and
the two men continue their conversation with the leading player who tells them that they are to present a
play before the court. Guildenstern asks that the player
give them some advice on what to do—he has been
there before and knows the temper of the court. The two

are filled with uncertainty. The following dialogue takes place:

> PLAYER: Uncertainty is the normal state. You're nobody special.
>
> GUILDENSTERN: But for God's sake what are we supposed to do?
>
> PLAYER: Relax. Respond. That's what people do. You can't go through life questioning your situation at every turn.
>
> GUILDENSTERN: But we don't know what's going on, or what to do with ourselves. We don't know how to *act*.
>
> PLAYER: Act natural! You know why you're here at least.
>
> GUILDENSTERN: We only know what we're told, and that's little enough. And for all we know it isn't even true.
>
> PLAYER: For all anyone knows, nothing is. Everything has to be taken on trust; truth is only that which is taken to be true. It's the currency of living. There may be nothing behind it, but it doesn't make any difference so long as it is honoured. One acts on assumptions.

The Player speaks as the worldly-wise man. Those of us who seek absolute answers, transcendent answers, have trouble with this mundane advice that since there is no certainty, one must act upon assumptions. It is this tentative quality which makes life such a nervous procedure. Great courage is required to endure the anxiety of living in an open age where "truth is only that which is taken to be true." We are reminded of Paul's insight that, in this life, we know only in part, for we see everything in a dark or distorted mirror. Modern people turn to an astrologer or a guru for direction, for clear answers to the major questions of existence. But they are forced to return again and again to the realization that "one acts on assumptions."

The thought comes to the two friends that they may have to go on always in uncertainty. But they recognize that there is an end to the torture—death. They see death as an answer to their problems, but do not welcome it. It is a depressing thought to contemplate being "in a box with a lid on it." The ambivalence in our feeling about death is brought out in a speech by Rosencrantz:

> You'd be helpless, wouldn't you? Stuffed in a box like that, I mean you'd be in there for ever. Even taking into account the fact that you're dead, it isn't a pleasant thought. *Especially* if you're dead, really . . . *ask* yourself, if I asked you straight off—I'm going to stuff you in this box now, would you rather be alive or dead? Naturally, you'd prefer to be alive. Life in a box is better than no life at all, I expect. You'd have a chance at least. You could lie there thinking—well, at least I'm not dead! In a minute someone's going to bang on the lid and tell me to come out. (*Banging the floor with his fists.*) "Hey you, whatsyername! Come out of there!"

He repeats that it is a depressing thought and makes the observation: "Eternity is a terrible thought. I mean, where's it going to end?" This is certainly one of the enigmas of human existence. Death is a fact of our experience—at least for other people. It is almost impossible for us to accept the fact of our own death. In the same way, eternity is a common idea but it is impossible for us to grasp it because everything we know has an end. Life based on only assumptions is a wearing experience, but we choose it over the "peace" of death.

Rosencrantz and Guildenstern finally meet Hamlet, but fail to ask him any important questions and find out nothing about him. The prince looks upon them as stool pigeons sent to spy upon him and he is careful to tell them nothing. It is obvious that they are wasting their time. Still, they cannot leave. They have been commanded to be at the court. They continue in uncertainty and frustration.

Again they meet with the actors and question the leading Player about the drama to be presented at court. He tells them it is a bloody melodrama, a slaughterhouse with eight corpses. Guildenstern then gives his opinion that melodramatic deaths on stage are too theatrical and do not bring real death home to anyone. The screaming, choking, and sinking to the knees are obvious actions that have little to do with honest human experience. He wonders if anyone can believe in a stage death. The Player answers that it is the only kind that people do believe in. They have been conditioned to it by many actors in many melodramas over the years.

The Player remembers that he had an actor once who was condemned to death for stealing. Permission was given to have the actor hanged in the middle of a play. It was thought that *this* death would be truly effective, the real article! But, as the Player relates:

He just *wasn't* convincing! It was impossible to suspend one's disbelief—and what with the audience jeering and throwing peanuts, the whole thing was a *disaster!*—he did nothing but cry all the time—right out of character—just stood there and cried. . . . Never again.

Audiences know what to expect, and that is all that they are prepared to believe in.

What happens when a generation has been conditioned to expect the conditions and "answers" of a structured society and that society has faded away? Can we comprehend "reality" for which we are not prepared? Are there styles in living and dying that determine how we shall do both? Is there such a thing as reality out there, beyond us, or is there only our conditioned reflexes to what happens? Do we see what is there or only what we have been prepared to see? This is a question that each one must answer for himself.

After the play has been presented at court, the king becomes doubly suspicious of Hamlet and decides to be rid of him. Therefore, the king persuades the two friends to accompany Hamlet to England with a sealed letter to the king. The letter is Hamlet's death warrant. Rosencrantz and Guildenstern find themselves on a ship headed for England. As the voyage continues, they discover the comfort of having the direction of their journey determined for them. Guildenstern makes this observation:

Yes, I'm very fond of boats myself. I like the way they're—contained. You don't have to worry about which way to go, or whether to go at all—the question doesn't arise, because you're on a *boat*, aren't you? . . . I think I'll spend most of my life on boats. . . . Free to move, speak, extemporise, and yet. We have not been cut loose. Our truancy is defined by one fixed star, and our drift represents merely a slight change of angle to it: we may seize the moment, toss it around while the moments pass, a short dash here, an exploration there, but we are brought round full circle to face again the single immutable fact—that we, Rosencrantz and Guildenstern, bearing a letter from one king to another, are taking Hamlet to England.

The figure of a boat becomes a symbol for an institution, a social structure, a settled philosophy of life, a national policy or any other form of human establishment. The individual can give his loyalty to this form, whatever it is, and find security in that now his direction is set and answers are given by an "authority." There is a certain amount of freedom within defined limits. A boat can take several tacks on its way to a final destination which is accepted. People in a totalitarian country find relief in having escaped from freedom with its isolation, uncertainty, competition, and lack of preordained direction. Within a democracy there are many small institutional dictatorships which provide this same kind of security—class, race, church, government, university, industry. Each institution has its regulations and its answers to hard questions.

Left alone, on shore without a boat, the two friends are forced to make decisions at every step. "We act on

scraps of information, . . . sifting half-remembered directions that we can hardly separate from instinct." As
they struggle to find their way, the prayer becomes:
"Give us this day our daily cue." But on the ship they
do not have to worry for the time being. The ship will
carry them along with all the others on board. All those
who are exhausted in their struggle with freedom know
the comfort that comes when one can relinquish the
helm to another steersman. The structures and institutions that make up an "establishment" offer to human
beings a haven for which they have devoutly wished.
Our problem today is that we are between cultures and
that our "boats" are in dry dock being overhauled. Few
reliable ships are sailing under trusted captains. We
have been thrust back into our human freedom, and it is
a frightening experience.

The two young men enjoy the security of the voyage
for a time and then begin to worry about what will happen to them when they arrive in England and have to
leave the ship. They will be plunged again into the unknown and will be forced to make decisions once more.
But then they remember that they have a letter to the
English king. As one says: "We've got a letter which
explains everything." Perhaps this letter will be as effective as the boat in giving them direction. After much
conversation, they open the letter and discover that it
commands the king of England to cut off Hamlet's head.
They are, of course, upset by this information but decide
it is destiny and they can do nothing about it.

During the night, while the two sleep, Hamlet takes

the letter, rewrites it and returns it to them. The next day, there is an attack on the ship by pirates. In the confusion, Hamlet escapes with the marauders and when order is reestablished, Rosencrantz and Guildenstern find themselves left on the ship bound for England without their charge. They wonder what will happen to them now. The security of the future seems to have been taken away with Hamlet. They decide to read the letter again and find, to their consternation, that the wording has been changed so that it now reads: "Without delay of any kind, should those bearers, Rosencrantz and Guildenstern, [be] put to sudden death—"

At this point, they discover the disadvantage of being on a boat. They cannot now escape their destination. They can leap overboard and drown or wait until the ship lands and be put to death. Being on a boat, they have lost their personal mobility. Guildenstern says quietly:

> Where we went wrong was getting on a boat. We can move, of course, change direction, rattle about, but our movement is contained within a larger one that carries us along as inexorably as the wind and current.

Rosencrantz wonders why it all happened. He feels that "they" had it in for the two companions right from the beginning. "Who'd have thought we were so important?" At this point, the Player, who with his troupe of actors is also on the ship, comes up and answers their question: "You are Rosencrantz and Guildenstern. That's enough." Two unknown little people are the objects of this plot of kings. They are not princes or royalty of any sort. The twentieth century has been called the century of the common man. Stoppard offers us two average persons who find this designation to be as fateful as social importance in other ages. In Western democratic culture when the individual began to emerge from the mass and to strive for recognition, he learned that he then must accept the position at the juncture of freedom and destiny which his newfound prominence created for him.

The ship sails on toward England—and execution for the two. The Player announces: "In our experience, most things end in death." The voyage of life is always toward death. It does not make much sense to mankind. The two friends return to their original confusion:

ROSENCRANTZ: What was it all about? When did it begin? Couldn't we just stay put? I mean no one is going to come on and drag us off. . . . They'll just have to wait. We're still young . . . fit . . . we've got years. . . . We've done nothing wrong! We didn't harm anyone. Did we? . . . All right, then. I don't care. I've had enough. To tell you the truth, I'm relieved. (*He disappears from view.*)
GUILDENSTERN: Our names shouted in a certain dawn. . . a message. . . . There must have been a moment, at the beginning, where we could have said—no. But somehow we missed it. . . . Well, we'll know better next time. Now you see me, now you—(*He disappears.*)

At the close of the play, the stage is lighted up and reveals the last scene from Shakespeare's *Hamlet*. The

king, queen, Laertes, and Hamlet are all dead. Horatio
is holding Hamlet. The two ambassadors from England
have appeared and one speaks lines from the original
drama:

> The sight is dismal;
> And our affairs from England come too late:
> The ears are senseless that should give us hearing,
> To tell him his commandment is fulfill'd,
> That Rosencrantz and Guildenstern are dead.
> Where should we have our thanks?

Stoppard's play ends in a question mark. As we look
back, we see that birth summons us into life. Names are
given. We are started on a journey whose destination is
never clear. We question each step of the way. We are
never really sure of our identity. We seem to be playing
roles in some kind of drama, but most of us are insig-
nificant characters and we wonder that the author
bothered to mention us in the cast or to give us lines
to speak. Death is a fact in life, but it is not a reality
for the living . . . not their own death. We find relief
in taking passage on various ships (or institutions)
during life, but this can be dangerous if the ship is
headed for the rocks or if our own destiny is to be settled
upon landing. Each of us carries a letter telling about
the final outcome of his life This letter is sometimes
called a biochemical time clock built into each of us.
It reveals our structural weaknesses and names the
natural cause of death if we can escape accidents. It is
fortunate that most of us cannot read the letter we carry.
Death comes as a mystery. It is as arbitrary and as
meaningless as the original call into life.

Tom Stoppard does not attempt to give a philosophical or religious interpretation to life. As has been said, he seeks to help us to understand what it "feels like" to live between cultures. Those who consider themselves educational or spiritual leaders in our day often find that they are subjected to the tyranny of answers. This is an inner tyranny which makes individuals feel that they must be able to give answers in order to justify their position among men. It is important, at our time in history, not to be caught in this tyranny. Karl Barth once said to ministers: "We cut a ridiculous figure as village sages—or city sages. As such we are socially superfluous. We do not understand the profession of the ministry unless we understand it as an index, a symptom, say rather an omen, of a perplexity which extends over the whole range of human endeavor, present and future."

Stoppard helps us to understand this perplexity. If we want to understand what it is like to be alive today, ponder the adventures and questions of Rosencrantz and Guildenstern. Our existence is set in the environment of a mystery. By attempting to give answers, we cut others off from the exercise of delving into the mystery, struggling with it, and receiving whatever response is waiting for them. A Canadian educator, J. Stanley Glenn, made a wise observation about Christian teaching: "[We are tempted] to accept a facile spirit which is capable of emptying the Bible and the best theology of content so that no mystery remains, no necessity of hard thinking, no rending of the heart, no suffering in order to understand, and no dying in order to live."

All our human strength and courage is required to

exist in freedom and to eschew easy answers which are false comforts. The German poet Rainer Maria Rilke once entreated his friends to be patient of all the unsolved problems of their hearts and to care for the questions themselves. He suggested that human beings should live in the questions and that, little by little, they would enter into the answers and live in them also. In our day, this advice is of the utmost importance.

When the Jewish leader Nicodemus came to Jesus by night to ask some of the questions that puzzled him, the answer he received was: "The wind blows where it wills, and you hear the sound of it, but you do not know whence it comes or whither it goes; so it is with every one who is born of the Spirit." Obviously, Jesus refused to stand under the tyranny of answers.

As we consider Tom Stoppard's play, are we able to "live in the questions"? This is the challenge of our age between cultures.

9
THE PERENNIAL
IDENTITY CRISIS

ARTHUR MILLER IS ONE OF THE MOST THOUGHTFUL
dramatists of our time. He is concerned about the moral
problems that appear as history unfolds in our culture.
He has become aware that human beings, and entire
societies, have to pay a price for every decision made.
He deals with this concern in his latest play entitled *The
Price*.

Miller is not a contemporary playwright. He is not
writing for the Theater of the Absurd. He is not an
avant-garde, radical writer dealing with the latest con-
fusions of lost souls trying to exist in an era between
cultures. He is not of the school of Beckett, Ionesco,
Genet, Albee, Pinter, and Stoppard. Miller's most recent
play has a story line and characters who speak sense as
they struggle with family problems and with questions
about their self-identity.

Arthur Miller is a product of the Great Depression of
the thirties. This event in American history made a deep
impression on him. He seems to believe that the depres-

sion made its mark on all Americans. He sees us as a secular, sensate society with little sense of transcendence. We are basically practical and materialistic. We have developed the belief that anything that succeeds is right. In crass terms, to succeed means to make money. When the country is affluent, all is well and we are doing what we are supposed to do. But when there is a depression, we are overwhelmed with a sense of failure and guilt. What have we done to deserve this punishment? How could this tragedy befall us?

Financial failure in our society has moral overtones. Only unworthy persons fail. To lose one's money is to lose everything. We seem to identify ourselves with our money. When the Great Depression struck, a number of people committed suicide and others were broken for life. They could not understand how they could live without their money. We give lip service to "spiritual values," but as a people we base our lives on material things.

ARTHUR MILLER / *The Price*

Miller's concern is for what happens to individuals or to a society when the tragedy of a depression wipes out that financial basis for identity and social worth. How does the next generation react? In his drama *The Price* we witness the story of the financial failure of a wealthy man, Mr. Franz, of New York City, and the reaction of his two sons, Victor and Walter. Victor, the younger son, remained at home to take care of his broken father. To do so, he gave up a promising career in science, left college and became a policeman in order to have a steady income. He lived with his father and, after his marriage, continued to support his father. Walter, the older one, refused to let the failure of his father stand in his way. He continued his medical studies, became a doctor, made a good deal of money, but sent home only a token amount of five dollars a month. In the play, we watch the two confront each other some sixteen years later when they arrive in the attic of a Manhattan brownstone to arrange for the sale of their parents' furniture. The confrontation seems to be between duty and selfishness. But there is a great deal of hidden material behind and beneath those simple opposites. Victor is bitter about the price he had to pay in order to be the dutiful son; Walter is deeply wounded by the price he had to pay for success and wealth, for he lost his wife through divorce, his children, and his health. He was hospitalized for three years with a "breakdown."

In this moral decision, which should the good man choose—duty or personal success? The Danish theologian, Søren Kierkegaard, once said of any important decision: do it or don't do it, you will regret both. In his drama, Arthur Miller does not give an answer. He does not side with Victor or Walter. He presents the confrontation and lets the audience struggle with the moral question. As a younger man, Miller suggested answers and took a definite moral stance. His experience in life seems to have led him to the place where he is no longer caught by the "tyranny of answers." He now lets the situation speak for itself and is not afraid to allow the paradoxes in human existence to appear. Recently he said to a friend: "I have no solution for the human race."

If we do not have a solution, what do we have? This drama is a careful analysis of the human perennial identity crisis found in the lives of Victor and Walter Franz. In the beginning, we meet Victor in his police uniform as he enters the attic of his father's brownstone house in New York City. The large attic room is filled with old, but obviously expensive, furniture. The building is about to be demolished and the furniture must be sold. While he is becoming reacquainted with his past, the wife, Esther, arrives and asks if he has been able to reach his brother, Walter. Victor admits that he cannot seem to reach Walter on the telephone. Esther is angry, and we realize that there is severe tension between the brothers. She urges Victor to bargain with the furniture dealer and be sure to get a good price.

Gregory Solomon, an elderly secondhand furniture dealer appears. He is affable and grandfatherly as well as very shrewd. He is almost ninety years old and enjoys getting to know his clients. Victor tries to hurry him to make an appraisal and give him a price. The old man puts him off and asks questions about the family history. He tells of his experience in business. He tries to explain to Victor that a "point of view" is necessary to understand the value of old furniture. The elaborate, ornate pieces in the attic are too large for modern apartments and suburban homes. Such furniture has little actual value today even though it was imported from Europe and was costly at the time of purchase. Another problem is that the furniture is so massive and well made that it will never break. Solomon says that the key word today is "disposable." The more easily you can throw something away, the more beautiful it is. Modern things are not made to last. People like to go shopping and buy new things. Victor's furniture is built for a century of wear; if one buys it, shopping is over. There are no more possibilities. Such considerations as these, of course, affect the price.

Victor finally tells Solomon about his father—that he was a millionaire who went broke within five weeks after the crash of '29. The event crushed him. He sat in the attic amid his furniture, which had to be moved out of the lower floors in order to rent them, and listened to his radio. He worked briefly at the Automat and delivered telegrams, but his life was over. Victor says that he himself had to drop out of school to keep the old man from starving to death.

Solomon makes a decision at last and offers Victor $1,100 for everything. The old dealer insists that it is a good price. Victor struggles for a moment and then agrees to take it. At this moment, Walter comes into the attic. He is in a hurry and explains that he just came to say hello and is not interested in the sale of the furniture—whatever satisfies Victor will be all right with him. The two brothers talk, and it comes out that Walter is divorced and that his children are doing poorly in school and that he has been sick, a nervous breakdown. Victor relates that his only child, Richard, is at M.I.T. on a full scholarship.

The brothers persuade Gregory Solomon to go into

the bedroom off the attic and let them talk together. Walter suggests that instead of selling the furniture, they might make a charitable contribution of it. They could have Solomon estimate its value at $25,000. Walter would take this as a tax deduction which would, in his tax bracket, save him about $12,000 which he would split with Victor. Under this plan, instead of getting $1,100, each brother would realize about $6,000. It appears that Solomon would be willing to make the required estimate for them. Victor is not sure he wants to have anything to do with such a deal—even though it is legal.

Walter leaves to talk further with Solomon in the bedroom and Victor and Esther are left alone. She tells him to take the money offered by Walter, to take it or she is through with him. Victor hesitates. Walter returns and the conversation continues about the past. Soon they are reliving old arguments. Victor accuses Walter of walking out on the family when the trouble came. Walter retaliates by telling Victor that he was a fool to allow himself to be caught in the situation by giving up his education and going to work as a policeman. The old wounds are opened again. The two men rage at one another until Walter walks out. Nothing has been accomplished. Victor closes the original deal with Solomon, takes his $1,100 and leaves with Esther to go to the movies. The old furniture dealer is left alone on the stage, listening to an old record of laughter on the ancient phonograph. He laughs heartily as the play ends.

A key line in the play is spoken by Walter toward the

end: "We invent ourselves." [40] By this is meant that each of us in his lifetime selects particular items out of many possibilities in his personality and develops a more or less integrated character. In this process, a number of interesting possibilities are left out. We integrate ourselves around a basic personal concern. We mourn the "death" of talents we omit because they do not support our basic concern. Charles Darwin was born with the capacity to appreciate great music. He decided to concentrate upon biology. As he grew older, he realized that he had lost his ability to understand music. His talent had atrophied. By selection and rejection of various parts of his personality, Darwin invented himself. In this play, Arthur Miller speculates on this phenomenon of human life and lets us see how it takes place in the lives of two brothers.

Victor, as a youth, was an excellent student and possessed a true talent in the field of science. It was recognized that he had more ability than his brother, Walter, in this direction. But when the depression struck and the family fortune disappeared, Victor decided to give up college, to stay home with his bewildered and lost father and to support the older man by taking any job he could find. After a number of odd jobs, he decided to join the police force because it offered security and a pension. When we meet him, Victor is fifty years old and is struggling with the decision to retire. His wife is un-

[40] This quotation and those which follow are from *The Price,* by Arthur Miller (The Viking Press, Inc.). Copyright © 1968 by Arthur Miller and Ingeborg M. Miller, Trustee. All rights reserved. Used by permission of The Viking Press, Inc.

happy and disappointed with their life because she feels
he has never "arrived." He had intended to be a policeman for a few years and then return to his "real" work
in science when good times appeared. During the Second
World War, he could have left the police force and
taken a high-paying position in war industry, but he
feared a depression after the war and decided to stick
with the police. When Walter offers him a good job as
an administrator in a hospital, a position where he would
stand between the medical men and the directors of the
hospital as an interpreter of each group to the other,
Victor turns it down with the cry that he does not understand modern science and cannot bring himself up to
date. As he looks back over his life, he recognizes that
he has, indeed, invented himself. He makes the statement: "It's that you have to make your move before you
understand what's involved, but you're stuck with the
results anyway."

Walter, on the other hand, started out with less native
ability than Victor but he has been an outstanding success in the eyes of the world. When the depression came,
he refused to give up his education and come home to support the family. He doggedly continued through college
and medical school. He became a surgeon and was soon
able to charge high fees to wealthy patients. He bought
into a number of nursing homes and made successful
investments. As he drove himself up the ladder of his
profession, he cut out of his personality all the capacity
for personal relationships. He paid little attention to his
father or brother. In his marriage, he saw little of his

wife and children. He invented himself as a hard-driving successful doctor and businessman. He saw medicine not so much as a profession but as a way to become financially secure. But the result was that his marriage was broken by divorce, his children enjoyed his money but had no interest in making anything of themselves, and his health disintegrated so that he had to spend three years in a mental hospital. When we meet him, Walter is in his fifties and is trying to resurrect some of his capacity for human relationship. He says he wants to become a true doctor, a professional who serves and saves people. But it is obvious that he has invented himself as a self-centered competitor and that this personality is his real one.

Victor makes the point for both of them when he explains to Walter why he cannot accept the position in the hospital:

> You can't walk in with one splash and wash out twenty-eight years. There's a price people pay. I've paid it, it's all gone. I haven't got it any more. Just like you paid, didn't you? You've got no wife, you've lost your family, you're rattling around all over the place. Can you go home and start all over again from scratch? This is where we are. Now, right here, now.

Arthur Miller delves into this matter of self-invention and points out that our decisions may be based upon illusions. We invent ourselves against a background of facts that may not be true. Our real motivation may be hidden from us as we select certain abilities to develop.

Victor may have thought he was being a dutiful son in giving up his education to support his father, but there might have been more subtle psychological reasons for his course of action. In the play, Miller tries to bring these hidden drives into the open.

Victor and Walter give two different responses to the same stimulus, the collapse of the family fortune. At the height of the prosperity of the 1920's, their father was worth about two million dollars. They lived in a large brownstone house in Manhattan. Their mother and father enjoyed the cultural life of the great city. Both sons were in good schools and expecting to attend excellent colleges. The future seemed secure. Then the depression struck and their world fell apart. This event was the most traumatic experience in their lives and it affected all their decisions from then on.

When Father Franz knew he had been wiped out financially, he brought his family together and announced that he was bankrupt. The mother and father were dressed in evening clothes for some affair. As Victor remembers the scene: "[He] made us all sit down; and he told us it was all gone. And she vomited all over his arms. His hand. Like thirty-five years coming up. And he sat there. And a look came onto his face. I'd never seen a man look like that."

One day this man had been head of a household and suddenly he was nothing. What his sons thought was love and loyalty turned out to be nothing but a straight financial arrangement. Their mother had once aspired to a musical career, she was a harpist, and had given it up to marry their father because he offered financial security. Suddenly she had neither her career nor security. This blow soon killed her. The father was left alone with the knowledge that his family had respected him as the source of financial security. When he could no longer provide this, he found that he had little value to them. This underlying concern for money is present in all Miller's thinking about the American way of life.

After the financial collapse had become accepted, the father moved his furniture into the attic of his handsome home and rented the rest of the house in an attempt to save what he could. But all he could collect went to pay his debts. He sat in the attic next to his radio and put in his time with a dazed and puzzled face. Victor went over to Bryant Park in the city. The grass was covered with men. They were not derelicts, but once solid citizens who had lost their jobs because of the depression. He noticed that they had shined shoes and good hats— that they were "busted businessmen, lawyers, skilled mechanics." He returned to his father's attic determined that this would not happen to his father. Victor recognized his duty and he intended to give up his own career in science to make life secure for his broken father. Walter was equally impressed by the scene, but he decided to break away and try to make it on his own.

The horror of the depression as he experienced it in his own home drove Victor to seek security at any cost but led him to think he was serving "duty" by remaining with his father. He became a policeman instead of a scientist. He chose security over risk. He thought he hated his work and longed for the time he could retire and begin a second career more to his liking and more in line with his real abilities. But when the time came that he could retire from the force, he found he could not make the decision. His wife, Esther, said to him: "Security meant so much to you." And as she looks back over their life together she notes: "It's like we never were anything, we were always about-to-be."

What Victor considers an act of duty turns out to be, in reality, an act of passive dependence. When he had to face a choice between risk and security, he inevitably chose security. This element in his personality comes clear in his relationship with Gregory Solomon, the furniture dealer. Victor does not attempt to bargain with Solomon over the price of the furniture. Esther tries to persuade Victor to bargain and meet Solomon man to man. She knows that he tends to belittle himself and anything he possesses. Victor says he will stand up to the dealer, but when a price is named by the old man, he accepts it.

In his conversation with Walter, it becomes clear that Father Franz understood that Victor needed to remain with him and not go on with his scientific education. There was a moment when Victor thought he might go on with his education and asked Walter to lend him $500 in order to get his degree. Walter refused him the loan, and it stunned Victor at the time. But Walter now tells him that he was ready to offer the money, that he had called the house and talked to their father:

> I spoke to Dad, and he told me you'd joined the Force. And I said he mustn't permit you to do a

thing like that. I said you had a fine mind, and with a little luck you could amount to something in science. That it was a terrible waste. And his answer was, "Victor wants to help me. I can't stop him." . . . So when he said that you wanted to help him, I felt somehow that it'd be wrong for me to try to break it up between you. It seemed like interfering.

Walter also reveals that the father was not absolutely broke, he had $4,000 left which Walter had invested for him. If he had wanted to, Father Franz could have lent Victor the money needed to complete his education. Victor claims he did not know of the existence of this money, but Walter says that his brother simply did not want to know about it. It becomes clear that Victor used the financial collapse of his father as a cover for his inner need to remain at home. He had the illusion that he was doing his duty as a loyal son and he was angry with Walter for walking out on his family responsibilities. But beneath the illusion was the reality of his own dependence which had been stirred into demanding action by the experience of the depression. He struggled with passive dependency all his life and called it filial duty.

This basic element of fear in Victor's personality has brought frustration to his wife. Esther feels that they have been cheated out of their rights in life. Walter has taken everything for himself and left Victor with nothing. She feels that Victor made his brother's whole career possible by taking care of their father and freeing Walter to go his own way. She believes there is such a thing as a moral debt involved. Victor scoffs at the idea and says that Walter would not know what they were talking about. Victor resents Walter's success and aloofness, but he does not know how to confront him. As Esther says of her husband, he is "indoctrinated with second place." When Victor doubts if the furniture is worth very much, Esther says: "Just because it is ours, why must it be worthless?" She wants her husband to stand up and be a man, to plunge into the world and win some of its prizes, to stop always protecting himself. As a realist and a practical person, Esther knows that in a secular, materialist culture, money is the one goal recognized universally. She points out to Victor what she thinks the trouble with them is: "We can never keep our minds on money! We worry about it, we talk about it, but we can't seem to *want* it. I do, but you don't. I really do, Vic. *I want money!*" But her experience with her husband makes her realize that he wants security more than anything else.

Walter felt the shock of the crash in 1929 as severely as did Victor, but his response was totally different. The collapse of their father terrified Walter, and he determined that it would never happen to him. Instead of making security his god, he enshrined success. Victor avoided what he called the "rat race," whereas Walter plunged into it with furious energy. He dedicated himself to beating the system by gaining money and prestige. He thought he was driven by ambition, but he found out that he was driven by fear as he remembered the horror of the depression and its effect on his father's life.

Walter understood what Victor missed in modern life —that one can attempt to avoid the rat race and try to live for "higher" things like duty, but that such escape is impossible because, as Victor finally admits: "There's no respect for anything but money." So Walter set out to get it. He explains himself this way:

> You start out wanting to be the best, and there's no question that you do need a certain fanaticism. There's so much to know and so little time. Until you've eliminated everything extraneous—including people. And of course the time comes when you realize that you haven't merely been specializing in something—something has been specializing in you. You become a kind of instrument, an instrument that cuts money out of people.

His profession was a way to make money, not to heal people. He was a success. When he used to visit his father in the attic, the older man looked upon him with pride and respect. Victor never received this look from his father regardless of all he had sacrificed for the man. But Walter's success did not bring him happiness. His disregard of people led him to alienate his family and made it impossible for him to have friends. His repressed anxieties began to make trouble for him and he broke down. In the mental hospital he began to see himself more clearly and to understand his inner motivation. He tries to express this to Esther and Victor:

> You get to see the terror—not the screaming kind, but the slow, daily fear you call ambition, and cautiousness, and piling up money.

When he was released from the hospital, Walter determined to change his way of life. He sold his three nursing homes (there is big money in the aged, in helpless, desperate children trying to dump their parents). He pulled out of the stock market. He began to give 50 percent of his time to city hospitals and he made medicine the center of his life. He says that he now feels alive for the first time.

Walter claims that he at last understands what Victor did. In the past, he could not understand why his brother would give up a promising future to stay home and support their father. But when he was sick, Walter realized that Victor had made a choice—had decided to follow duty instead of success in the world. He says to Victor: "You wanted a real life. And that's an expensive thing; it costs." Now he wants to be friends with his brother, but Victor is still suspicious of him and will not shake hands and forget the past. He insists that Walter walked out on a responsibility and cannot undo it by simply coming around and saying that he is sorry.

Walter tries to explain to Victor that the situation did not have the moral qualities now extolled by his brother. He points out that Victor was actually exploited by their father. The love that Victor talks about was an illusion, a screen he erected to hide the unhappy reality. Walter bores in with these searing words:

> Were we really brought up to believe in one another? We were brought up to succeed, weren't we? Why else would he [Father Franz] respect me so and not you? . . . Was there ever any love

here? . . . What was unbearable is not that it all
fell apart, it was that there was never anything here.
. . . There was nothing here but a straight financial arrangement. That's what's unbearable. And you
proceeded to wipe out what you saw.

What is the truth? Each brother has his own version of
what took place. Walter protects himself by saying that
there was no great moral responsibility involved, only a
financial arrangement. Victor believes that there was
love in the family and that he had to stay home and care
for his father. Walter's response to the crash was to look
out for himself, to make himself invulnerable. He says
he changed his way of life after his breakdown, but we
witness his manner of bargaining with the furniture
dealer, Gregory Solomon.

When Walter arrives in the attic, Victor has already
made an agreement with Solomon for $1,100. Walter
disregards this agreement and begins another tack with
Solomon. His suggestion that the dealer give them an
estimate of the highest retail value of the furniture, so
that they could then donate the furniture to the Salvation Army, Walter taking an income tax deduction and
splitting the amount saved with Victor, makes it clear
that Walter is far from penniless in his new way of life
and that he thinks in terms of "deals" when faced with
a new situation. His justification for his suggestion is the
well-worn one: "It's done all the time. It's a dream world,
but it's legal." Walter concludes his plan by saying: "It's
really the only sensible way to do it."

Victor is suspicious of everything Walter says. He

refuses to shake hands and fit into his brother's plans. There is no meeting between them. Walter rushes out of the attic with the words: "You will never, never again make me ashamed!"

If Victor's illusion is that he served duty when he actually was seeking security as a dependent person, Walter's illusion is that he has changed his way of life and is now a free man serving others as a doctor. When we consider what happened, Walter's willingness to leave home and go out on his own was an act of courage and independence, although it was based upon the same fear of failure that motivated Victor.

Arthur Miller seems to be saying that there are two incompatible moral attitudes present in this situation, and in our whole society. The depression has had a tremendous effect upon the American character. In a culture where money is central, the sudden collapse of financial security drives people into fanatical ways in an attempt to preserve themselves. Dependent persons withdraw from the risks of the rat race and seek security in a safe occupation, even though it may stunt their growth as personalities; independent persons plunge into the rat race with a grim determination that they will come out ahead and thus find safety in "making it." One must choose between these paths and pay a price. Both of these brothers paid high prices for their choices.

On the surface, human beings seem to be torn between moral responsibility and greedy self-seeking. But in this play we realize that there are unconscious motivations which drive them on. Victor and Walter were both driven by fear of failure, a fear made vivid by the financial collapse of their father. Their reactions to fear were different but common to so many in our society. Miller suggests that there is no meeting between the two styles of life. Victor is morally indignant at Walter's callous self-seeking; Walter is contemptuous of Victor's unrealistic sentimentality. The only possibility for reconciliation is for them both to recognize that their choices and their lives result from a common experience of fear. What does this have to say to the present antagonisms in American life?

In this play, Miller includes an important fourth character—Gregory Solomon, the furniture dealer who is almost ninety years old. He carries his discharge from the British Navy to prove his advanced age. Victor had found his name in an old telephone book, in the yellow pages, and asked him to come to the attic and make an estimate on the furniture. Although Solomon is practically retired, he agrees to come and arrives eager to do business. He loves the process of making a deal and has missed being in active business. He is knowing, shrewd, understanding, and sociable. He is also the first thoroughly humorous character to appear in any play by Arthur Miller.

Solomon is here to act as a contrast to the brothers as well as to the modern American spirit. He is out of another tradition. He has a European background and has had a rich experience in various cultures. He has known joy and tragedy and embraced both as part of life. Above all, he is not afraid of failure. The deep motivating factor of fear in the personalities of the two brothers is absent in Gregory Solomon.

He likes to become acquainted with his clients. He does not enjoy coming right to the point in a business transaction. Victor keeps trying to hurry him into making an estimate about the value of the furniture; Solomon puts him off and wants to talk about the family background and to discuss what is happening in the area of crime, since Victor is a policeman. Solomon explains: "What happens to people is always the main element to me." Victor, in some exasperation, says that he is not sociable and just wants the old dealer to come to a price. Solomon asks with surprise: "You don't want we should be buddies?" Then he continues to talk about his own life and to ask questions about Victor's life.

When Victor insists upon hurrying him, Solomon stubbornly resists and says that he cannot do business unless he knows the other person and can believe in him. Victor reminds him that it is simply a business matter and he wants to hear a price. Solomon shakes his head.

> Mister, I pity you! What is the matter with you people! . . . Nothing in the world you believe, nothing you respect—how can you live? Let me give you a piece of advice—it's not that you can't believe nothing, that's not so hard—it's that you still got to believe it. *That's* hard. And if you can't do that, my friend, you're a dead man!

With all his interest in socializing, Solomon is a tenacious competitor in business. When Walter meets him, he is at once impressed by the old man's drive. But this amazing energy is not triggered by fear, either recognized or unconscious, but by a great enjoyment of existence and interaction with people. Solomon inspects the furniture and realizes at once that Father Franz was a wealthy man. He asks Victor how his father could go broke with so much obvious wealth. Victor answers that it took only five weeks for the entire fortune to disappear. Solomon asks about making a comeback, and Victor says that his father was stunned and just sat there in the attic and listened to the radio. He took some odd jobs now and then, but he did not recover from the blow. Solomon asks: "What was the matter with him?" Victor replies that some men just don't bounce.

This is incredible to Gregory Solomon. In the tradition out of which he came, failure and success followed one another, and men dealt with them as they appeared. Solomon says to Victor: "Listen, I can tell you bounces. My life is a regular basketball. I went busted 1932. Then 1923 they also knocked me out. The Panic of 1904, 1898. But to lay down like *that* . . ." In his personal life, Solomon has been married four times and he suffered through the suicide of a beloved daughter. He explains: "You see, all my life I was a terrible fighter—you could never take nothing from me. I pushed, I pulled. I struggled in six different countries."

Victor and Walter, like their father before them, do not have the "bounce" of a Gregory Solomon, or the realism. The old man knows how to live and not be destroyed by adversity. He knows how to grasp each moment and find elements of interest in it. Arthur Miller suggests that America has built up an illusion about history and human existence—that the nation, and individuals in it, have to succeed. "America has never lost a war," proclaim the politicians. We tend to think of ourselves as different from other countries. Our ancestors escaped from the vices of the old Europe and came to these shores to create a new, virtuous way of life. The early churchmen of the colonies spoke of this land as "God's new Israel." The American Dream of the land of freedom and equality developed, and we believed we deserved success because we were good. The Great Depression and the wars of the twentieth century have unnerved us. These tragedies "cannot" happen to us! There are many people, like Victor and Walter Franz, who are driven by an inner panic either to avoid the rat race or to compete successfully in it. Life is not enjoyable to them and they have little zest for it. Gregory Solomon appears in this play to remind us of our roots in an older tradition where one faces many defeats and comes back to enjoy life again.

At the close of the play, Solomon remains behind after the other three have left. As Victor is going, the following dialogue takes place:

VICTOR: I'm glad to have met you, Solomon.
SOLOMON: Likewise. And I want to thank you.
VICTOR: What for?
SOLOMON: (*With a glance at the furniture*) Well . . . who would ever believe I would start such a thing again? . . . But go, I got a lot of work here.

VICTOR: Good luck with it.
SOLOMON: Good luck you can never know till the
last minute, my boy.

Alone on the stage, Solomon looks at the furniture piled
around him and is somewhat oppressed by it. He moves
slowly to the ancient phonograph and turns the crank.
Then he plays the Laughing record in which two co-
medians do nothing but howl with laughter. Solomon sits
back in Father Franz's big chair and relaxes. He smiles,
he chuckles as he remembers the old vaudeville turn, he
begins to laugh. He leans back in the chair, laughing with
tears in his eyes as the curtain falls.

Again, we have here an analysis of the American
temper. If there is to be communication between culture
and counter culture or between the Christian community
and the surrounding society, it is imperative that we
listen to the voice of the artist-playwright who is sensitive
to our way of life and tells it as it is.

10
THE COST
OF INTEGRITY

THE MAN OF INTEGRITY HAS A DIFFICULT TIME IN A SECULAR age which puts its emphasis upon adjustment and the process of coming to terms with things as they are. To exist in civilization a man must be prepared to surrender certain personal objectives and ideals. To avoid constant conflict, men have to learn to compromise and to fit into the general social scheme about them. The complete individualist finds himself isolated and rejected by his fellows. The need for compromise makes each of us somewhat neurotic, as Sigmund Freud pointed out in his *Civilization and Its Discontents.* The "practical" approach to life has made us downgrade the concept of character or moral integrity in our time.

Education in our society seeks to provide knowledge and skills to young people so that they can earn a living. There is also a "civic" role in our schooling that attempts to mold young people into a conforming pattern so that they will fit into our "way of life." There has been little concern of late for the development of strength of character among the young so that they will be able to function as free, responsible human beings when they reach maturity. Morality is now recognized as situational and ethical standards are understood sociologically. It is not fashionable to be a person of character.

Yet men and women in today's world know instinctively that there is a desperate need for character and integrity if the human race is to survive. If character is ignored, concern over human behavior will tend to find its only expression in demands for "law and order." Lack of integrity will lead us into some form of police state and totalitarian repression.

The dramatists are well aware of this important need in our society. They have searched for persons of character and have come up with two famous personages to act as symbols and as inspiration for us: Thomas More of Britain and Miguel de Cervantes of Spain. It is of interest that both these men are out of the somewhat distant past. Is it impossible to find men of character in our modern society?

In their own times and countries, More was considered a dangerous public enemy who had to be executed, and Cervantes created Don Quixote who was looked upon by his contemporaries as a senile fool. But the political heretic and the social nonconformist have come down to us as admirable men of integrity.

Thomas More lived from 1478 until 1535 when he was beheaded for treason against his king, Henry VIII of England. He was educated at Oxford and combined medieval and Renaissance views in his philosophy of life.

He was well acquainted with humanism and was a close friend of Erasmus but was also a faithful Catholic who upheld the cause of the pope and the Roman Catholic theological system of his day. As a young man, he was deeply concerned with the development of his own character. At one time, he sought to follow the medieval path toward the ascetic life in order to purge himself of worldliness and the temptation toward easy living. He wore a painful hair shirt, whipped himself every Friday and on other fast days, lay on the bare ground with a log for a pillow, and allowed himself to sleep only four or five hours a night. He lived under this regimen from the time he was nineteen until he was twenty-three. He left this life of ascetic discipline only when he felt that he was in control of his body and mind.

More studied law and entered Parliament. He was an extremely able young man and rapidly advanced in the political realm. He was made undersheriff of London and, later, master of requests and a member of the privy council. At the age of forty-three he was knighted and as Sir Thomas More was appointed subtreasurer to the king. He rose from this position to be Speaker of Parliament and finally was made Lord Chancellor of England. In all these positions he proved himself to be a man of absolute honesty. When the inevitable bribes were offered, he consistently rejected them. He even refused to accept gifts from friends when he was in financial difficulty after retiring from his chancellorship. It was because of the moral quality of his life that Samuel Johnson said of More: "He was the person of the greatest virtue these islands ever produced."

ROBERT BOLT / *A Man for All Seasons*

In the play *A Man for All Seasons,* by Robert Bolt, we find More as a man who cannot go along with the will of his king because of his conscience. There is a scene in which Henry VIII attempts to persuade Thomas More to agree with him that he ought to divorce his queen. More insists that he would like to please his sovereign, but that he cannot do so with a clear conscience. The king flares up and insists that he must have a son and heir and that it is his *duty* to put away the present queen in order to have a wife who can give him a son. Henry declares that everyone else can see his point and asks More why he is so obstinate. Thomas More replies that if everyone else is agreed, why does the king need his poor support? Then Henry makes his complaint clearly:

> Because you are honest. What's more to the purpose, you're known to be honest. There are those like Norfolk [a loyal nobleman] who follow me because I wear the crown, and there are those like Master Cromwell who follow me because they are jackals with sharp teeth and I am their lion, and there is a mass that follows me because it follows anything that moves—and there is you." [41]

At this point, let us look briefly at the argument of the play itself.

A Man for All Seasons celebrates the tragic grandeur

[41] This quotation and those which follow are from *A Man for All Seasons,* by Robert Bolt (Random House, Inc.). Copyright © 1960, 1962, by Robert Bolt. All rights reserved. Used by permission of Random House, Inc.

of the man of ultimate conscience, Thomas More. In an
era of secular cynicism, the *Playboy* Philosophy of he-
donism, and casual morality, More is a shining beacon of
firmly established honor.

Thomas More, a sixteenth-century, staunch Catholic
layman, became the first lay Chancellor of England. As
a man of faith and conscience, he refused to turn his
back on Rome and to agree to Henry VIII's divorce of
Catherine and subsequent marriage to Anne Boleyn.
Nor would he back his king in his move to become
supreme head of the Church of England when Henry
VIII broke with Rome in order that he might gain ec-
clesiastical freedom to marry Anne. Others of position in
the court and church were rearranging their thinking in
order to accommodate the king. Pressure was brought to
bear on Sir Thomas to imitate them. He refused to for-
sake his private conscience. Cardinal Wolsey complained
to him: "You're a constant regret to me, Thomas. If you
could just see facts flat on, without that horrible moral
squint, with just a little common sense, you could have
been a statesman."

As a man of conscience he was no sainted fool. He
sought a way to keep his integrity, and at the same time
to avoid being attacked and made to suffer. He possessed
no martyr complex. As a lawyer, he decided that his
safety lay in silence. Quietly he resigned the chancellorship and retired to his home. He refused to express his
strong objections to the king's actions. But his silence did
not satisfy his enemies. They claimed that More's reputation was so great that his "silence" was bellowing up

and down Europe. Regardless of his silence, his enemies had him arrested and imprisoned in the Tower of London until he would either renounce his opposition to the king or sign the Act of Succession.

More's friends and family tried to persuade him to play the game by swearing an oath to the king as head of the Church of England. But Sir Thomas would not relent: "When a man takes an oath, . . . he's holding his own self in his own hands. Like water. And if he opens his fingers *then*—he needn't hope to find himself again."

The author of the play, Robert Bolt, wants us to recognize that a man is free to make decisions about his own life. In our day we are told that human actions are caused by unconscious factors or by environmental influences. Man is a puppet manipulated by psychological and sociological strings. Thomas More denies this view by insisting that he, with his own mind and willpower, has chosen where he will stand and what he will do. His words make this clear: "I will not give in [and take the oath] because I oppose it—I do—not my pride, not my spleen, nor any other of my appetites, but *I* do—*I!*" Where are the men and women of today who dare to do their own thinking and conscientiously oppose popular views?

In the pressure brought upon More to conform to the position of the king, we see the dim shadow of the coming totalitarian state of the twentieth century. His enemies accuse Sir Thomas of conceited selfishness. They insist he ought to consider his place "in the State! Under

the King! In a great native country!" He defends himself
by standing upon his individuality and his honor: "Is it
my place to say 'good' to the State's sickness? Can I help
my King by giving him lies when he asks for truth?" It
requires a strong man to hold out for the truth he sees
when such truth is considered unpatriotic!

Finally brought to trial for treason, More is falsely
accused and condemned to death, although he kept his
silence to the end. When asked by his judge if he has
anything to say, More replies:

> I am a dead man. You have your desire of me.
> What you have hunted me for is not my actions,
> but the thoughts of my heart. It is a long road you
> have opened. For first men will disclaim their hearts
> and presently they will have no hearts. God help the
> people whose Statesmen walk your road.

This prophetic word is aimed at thought control,
brainwashing, subliminal persuasion, and all the other
forms of coercion developed by totalitarian regimes to
create and enforce conformity. Thomas More was beheaded as a high traitor to the king he loved but could
not betray by telling lies. He is an authentic tragic hero.
His moral strength is the backbone of every nation in
every century. He is, indeed, a man for all seasons and
all nations.

In the play, there is a man easily recognizable by us.
Called "The Common Man," he plays many minor roles
and comments on the action. He lives by his horse sense
and looks out for himself. He is not above accepting a
bribe; he has an easy conscience. After More's execution,
The Common Man speaks to us.

I'm breathing. . . . Are you breathing, too? . . .
It's nice, isn't it? It isn't difficult to keep alive, friends
—just don't *make* trouble—or if you must make
trouble, make the sort of trouble that's expected.
Well, I don't need to tell you that. Good night. If
we should bump into one another, recognize me.

Unfortunately, it is only too easy to recognize him!

Obviously, the world needs The Uncommon Man who
possesses a character that is both responsible and free.
More believed himself to be a man hunted for the personal thoughts of his heart, not for his actions. Modern
people live in fear of this same kind of hunting. Present-
day electronic developments make eavesdropping on
private citizens easily possible. Ramsey Clark, when he
was Attorney General of the United States, made the
statement: "If we create today traditions of spying on
people when they do not know it, it may not be too far
distant when a person can hardly think, much less speak
his mind to any other person without fear of police or
someone else knowing his thoughts or words."

DALE WASSERMAN/*Man of La Mancha*

Another approach to the man of integrity is found in the
musical dramatization of *Don Quixote* by Dale Wasserman.[42] Here we find the concept of human hope related
to the importance of character. Miguel de Cervantes, the
author of *Don Quixote*, is, like his famous literary creation,
a man of La Mancha. Cervantes was well acquainted

[42] *Man of La Mancha: A Musical Play*, by Dale Wasserman,
lyrics by Joe Darion (Random House, Inc., 1966).

with trouble. His life was a series of catastrophes and yet he retained his vision of what human existence could be. He had a varied career in the world as a soldier, playwright, actor, and tax collector. Frequently he found himself in prison for offenses related to his obedience to his conscience. It was in his later years that he created his testament to human integrity and hope which is called *Don Quixote.*

Alonso Quijana, in Cervantes' novel, was gaunt and growing old, but his eyes burned with the fire of inner vision. In his retirement, he read books day and night. These books were much like the popular works of our time, filled with descriptions of human deceptions and man's bloody aggressions against other men. Anger and indignation filled the old man's mind until he determined to become a knight-errant and to ride into the world to right all wrongs. He chose for himself the lordly name of Don Quixote and invited his neighbor, Sancho Panza, to be his squire.

To relatives and friends, the two men seemed utterly foolish or insane. But to Don Quixote his vision was the most real thing in his life. He had studied the days of chivalry from his youth. He knew intimately the code and the customs of the knight. He set out not so much to *play* a role as to *become* it. He refused to surrender to the emotional and spiritual aridity of his time. He set out to pit his inner hopes and dreams against the vulgar and dehumanizing influences of his era . . . or any era.

Quixote is asked to see facts as they are and he replies that "facts are the enemy of truth." In the musical

play, *Man of La Mancha,* Cervantes, speaking as himself
and not as his character Don Quixote, elaborates on the
meaning of this. He insists that there is a reality beyond
the factual. This is considered sheer folly to those of a
scientific-sensate culture like our own. The old man declares he has seen life as it is . . . full of pain, misery,
and hunger. He has observed cruelty beyond belief. He
has heard the raucous singing in taverns and heard the
moans from ragged beggars on the streets. Once he was
a soldier and he watched his comrades fall in battle or
he saw them die more slowly under lashing by whips in
Africa. He remembers that he held some of them in his
arms at the final moment. He recalls that although these
men saw life as it was, they died despairing without any
gallant last words. While he held them, their eyes were
filled with confusion as they whimpered the question,
"Why?" He does not think they asked why they were
dying, but why they had lived.

Against this life-denying "reality," Quixote asserted
his vision of compassionate, justice-serving chivalry . . .
a kind of madness or foolishness, perhaps, and yet a
saving grace. There is a paragraph in Paul's second
letter to the Christians at Corinth which reminds us of
Quixote's quest:

No wonder we do not lose heart! Though our
outward humanity is in decay, yet day by day we
are inwardly renewed. Our troubles are slight and
short-lived; and their outcome an eternal glory
which outweighs them far. Meanwhile our eyes are
fixed, not on the things that are seen, but on the

things that are unseen: for what is seen passes away;
what is unseen is eternal. (II Cor. 4:16-18.) [43]

Jesus came preaching, "The kingdom of God is at
hand." This Kingdom is the realm of truth beyond the
realm of fact. It is the realm in which the will of God
is done, where true compassion is the style of life, where
each individual has dignity. Jesus came as a prophet of
hope. Modern man is in desperate need of that message
today. Contemporary man feels lost and meaningless.
Henry David Aiken asks, "If the world does not care who
I am, how indeed can I think of *myself* as an enduring
person, a continuing center of loyalties, responsibilities
and human roles?" [44]

Man of La Mancha, a drama based on Cervantes' life
and his novel, *Don Quixote,* takes place in a prison at
Seville, Spain, at the end of the sixteenth century. In the
play we see the large common room of a stone prison
vault with a stairway like a drawbridge rising to a door
in the middle of the ceiling. The room swarms with
criminals and vagabonds. They have developed their
own prison society with leaders and servants. The door
opens, the stairway descends, and two men, Cervantes
and his servant, are thrust into the vault. They are immediately set upon by the other prisoners and robbed of
their possessions. We learn that Cervantes had been
jailed because, as an official tax collector, he had had the

[43] From *The New English Bible: The New Testament.* © The
Delegates of the Oxford University Press and The Syndics of the
Cambridge University Press, 1961, 1970.
[44] From "The New Morals," *Harper's Magazine,* February,
1968.

audacity to tax a church . . . or, as his servant put it, he had foreclosed on a church! This act gains him a measure of acceptance from the other prisoners. Nevertheless, they put him on trial in the prison and accuse him of being an idealist, a bad poet, and an honest man. Cervantes defends himself by acting out a story that he has written, the account of the adventures of Alonso Quijana who became Don Quixote.

In marvelous fashion, we are taken on the adventures by the miracles of music and the imagery of words. He fights with and is badly mauled by a giant who has been turned into a windmill by an enemy. Longing to be dubbed a knight, he seeks out a castle that actually is a most ordinary inn filled with rough muleteers served by a slatternly young woman. Don Quixote enters the shabby tavern and addresses the muleteers as gentle knights; he calls the uncouth serving girl a fair chatelaine. He announces that if any of them require assistance, they have but to speak and his right arm will be at their service. Turning to the serving girl, he is struck by what he takes to be her beauty and purity. She tells him that her name is Aldonza, but he insists that she is no other than the Lady Dulcinea and that she shall be his lady for whom he shall win great victories. The poor girl is bewildered and somewhat contemptuous of the old man.

A traveling barber comes that way, carrying his shaving equipment and wearing his brass basin on his head to protect him from the hot sun. Don Quixote recognizes the basin as the Golden Helmet of Mambrino. He insists that when this famous helmet is worn by one of noble

heart it protects him from all wounds. Accusing the barber of stealing the famous headgear, the old self-styled
knight draws his sword and frightens the man into giving
him the basin which he claps on his own head. During
the rest of his chivalric career he proudly wears the
Golden Helmet.

Don Quixote persuades the innkeeper, or "the Lord of
the Castle," to dub him a knight. In preparation for the
ceremony, he spends a night in solemn vigil reminding
himself of the true meaning of knighthood. He determines to call nothing his own except his soul, not to love
what he is but what he may yet become, not to seek
pleasure because he might have the misfortune to over-
take it, to look toward the future rather than the past, to
be just to all men and courteous to all women and,
finally, to live under the inspiration of his lady, Dulcinea,
for whom great deeds can be accomplished.

During his vigil and amid his musings, Aldonza has
entered the courtyard. Angrily, she asks him why he calls
her "Dulcinea." He insists it is her name and that he
knows her despite her disguise as a scullery maid; he
claims that he has known her all his life, known her virtue and nobility of spirit. She cannot understand him and
asks why he does such ridiculous things.

Quixote answers that he hopes to add some measure of
grace to the world. Bitterly Aldonza states flatly that the
world is a dungheap and that human beings are only
maggots that crawl on it. The aged don insists that she
knows better in her heart. But she retorts that what is in
her heart will get her halfway to hell and that he is about

to receive a savage beating for his nonsense. Quixote shrugs and says quietly that whether he wins or loses doesn't matter . . . that the only important thing is that he follow his quest. When the now curious woman asks him what that means, the old knight sings the famous ballad of "The Quest" in which he proclaims his credo that the world will be a better place because one man, scorned and beaten by the world, still struggled on with all his strength to reach the unreachable star.

Very seriously Aldonza approaches the inspired old man and asks him to look at her, just once, as she really is. He gazes into her coarse and ruined face and tells her gently that he sees beauty and purity. He declares that he sees the woman that every man holds a secret inside himself. Once more he calls her Dulcinea. She moans and runs from him, on her way to keep an appointment with one of the muleteers.

The next morning, the innkeeper stumbles through his role of Lord of the Castle and dubs the old wanderer a knight, giving him the added title, "Knight of the Woeful Countenance." Now, Quixote is ready to resume his chivalric life of adventure.

But back in his home at La Mancha the family is greatly disturbed by his strange actions. His reputation for bizarre behavior has reached the attention of his neighbors. His niece is engaged to be married to a learned man, Dr. Sansón Carrasco, and she is afraid that the match may be called off because her uncle has become the laughingstock of the region. The family decides to take desperate measures to bring the old man back to his senses. They visit him and try words of persuasion. He will hear none of them. He insists that his vision of "true life" is far more real than their so-called factual reality.

Not long after, Don Quixote encounters another knight who is tall and terrifying and wears fantastic armor. The ferocious stranger insults and challenges him by calling him a charlatan, a foolish pretender, and a childish dreamer. Don Quixote recognizes the terrifying specter as his great enemy, the Enchanter. The old knight tears off his left gauntlet and flings it at the challenger's feet as the gage of battle. The enemy drives Quixote into a rage when he calls Dulcinea an alley cat. But as the Knight of the Woeful Countenance rushes forward into the fray, the other man reverses his shield, the inside of which is so highly polished that it shines like a mirror which blinds and bewilders Quixote. The enemy's two attendants do the same with their shields, and the old knight reels from one mirror to another, always facing his own image. The Enchanter cries out for Don Quixote to look into the mirror of reality and to see things as they actually are. What does he see in the mirror? Not a gallant knight, but an aging fool . . . a madman dressed for a masquerade . . . a clown! In a powerful voice, the strange knight orders Quixote to drown in the mirror, to go deep, to admit that his lady is a trollop and that his dream is the nightmare of a disordered mind.

Broken by this cruel tactic, Don Quixote falls to his knees. Beaten and weeping, he collapses. The Enchanter removes his closed helmet, revealing himself to be none other than Dr. Carrasco. He explains that he was forced to use this "shock treatment" to shatter the old man's vision and to bring him back to "himself."

The last scene is played in the bedroom of the house in La Mancha where the old man, "cured" of his knighthood, lies dying. He is visited by Sancho Panza and, against the wishes of the family, by Aldonza. Timidly she approaches the bed and is amazed when Senor Alonso Quijana does not seem to know her. She calls him Don Quixote but he does not respond. She pleads with him to remember. He asks why it is important. She answers that everything depends upon his remembering . . . her whole life. She says that he spoke to her and that everything was different. Trying to stir his memory, she says that he looked at her and that he called her by the name of Dulcinea. She begs him to bring back the dream of Dulcinea . . . the bright and shining glory of Dulcinea. This seems to reach the old man and he begins to respond. She reminds him of his great quest and repeats to him the heroic words of his song. He gathers strength and once more becomes Don Quixote! He calls for his armor and his sword. He shouts for Sancho to join him for more adventures. He rises from his bed and strides about the room. Suddenly he falters and falls. He is dead. All are stunned.

Sancho breaks the silence by stating flatly that he is dead. Aldonza says quietly that he seemed like a good man, even though she did not really know him. Then she remarks to Sancho Panza that Don Quixote is not dead and exhorts him to believe. He starts to call her

Aldonza, but she stops him and says that her name is Dulcinea.

At this point the story of Don Quixote is broken into by the arrival of the officers of the Inquisition who have come to take the author, Cervantes, to his trial. The door opens, the stairway descends into the dungeon, monks and soldiers appear from above. Cervantes' prison friends wish him well. He ascends the stairs between the lines of hooded men and soldiers.

This secular version of the man of hope is a shadow of the Christian man of faith. Both seem like clowns and madmen to the world of facts, but they have a vision of a kingdom of justice and compassion desperately needed by men of all ages. Without that vision, life is absurd and its goal the grave.

In an article in *Look* magazine, the late Dr. James Pike explained why he had decided to leave the church. The core of his message was that he had lost "believing hope." He said that the subtle change from hope to no hope had finally become clear to him and that he had no alternative but to cut himself away from the church he had served for a quarter of a century. He implied that without believing hope one cannot function as a member of the Christian community.

To those whose hope is ebbing—or seemingly gone—comes the proclamation of the Christian faith that, to quote Jürgen Moltmann: "Everything is still full of possibilities." This rising German theologian pleads with us to recognize that "Christianity is . . . hope, forward looking and forward moving, and therefore also revolutionizing and transforming the present." He warns us to be careful not to "cancel the wayfaring character of hope."

Don Quixote looked into the face of Aldonza and saw the purity and shining glory of Dulcinea. His vision of her transformed her life from despair to hope. The encounter with the living Christ in the authentic Christian community creates the same transformation on a far deeper level. Man experiences a "new creation," a "new being." Jesus looked upon ordinary men and women and saw children of God.

Don Quixote had a dream of what life *might be* if chivalry could be reinstated; Jesus had a clear vision of what life ultimately *is* in the sight of God. That vision is the source of our believing hope.

Both Thomas More and Don Quixote (or Cervantes) lived in terms of a moral code and a faith that were not fashionable among the common people of their times. Today the two plays based upon the lives of these men of conscience have proved vastly popular across our nation. There is a deep hunger for integrity and hope in an age that celebrates in so much of its life confusion and absurdity.